About the Author

Nikita Catherine is from Tipperary, Ireland, growing up not far from the original homestead of this story's main characters. She is their great-granddaughter, by their son, Billy, and his wife, Kitty. She is a huge bookworm—fiction and history being her favourite. She based a lot of this book on the anecdotes and stories told to her by her grandmother, Kitty, on how her great-grandparents lived and raised their family in difficult circumstances, and on the stories of what her grandfather got up to with his siblings and kids. She has a diploma in photography—preferring portrait and landscape.

The Tailor's Daisy

Nikita Catherine

The Tailor's Daisy

Olympia Publishers
London

www.olympiapublishers.com
OLYMPIA PAPERBACK EDITION

A CIP catalogue record for this title is
available from the British Library.

ISBN: 978-1-80074-498-1

First Published in 2022

Olympia Publishers
Tallis House
2 Tallis Street
London
EC4Y 0AB

Printed in Great Britain

Dedication

For my nanny, Kitty Thompson. Missing my partner in crime.

Acknowledgements

First of all, thank you to my nanny for telling me most of these stories—I hope I did them justice. I wish you could have seen your name in print. Thank you to my mam for telling me the stories of mischief no one dared tell my nanny, helping me create the dynamic in Joe and Mary-Kate's children. Thanks to my family for their support. Thanks to all of my friends for their invaluable encouragement, especially Stephen who read a very rough and confusing draft of this. Thanks to all my extended family, many of whom inspired stories in this book. And finally thank you to the teacher, who on my last day in her school told me she would read a book by me someday—I never forgot that.

Inspired by True Stories

1

No matter how hard I gripped the top of my bag, I could not get it to open. Standing it on the top of my boots, I rubbed my hands together to try and warm them up. Bits of dirt rolled off them and they made a loud sandpaper noise. No point in breathing on them, I would probably just make them even colder.

"Any faster and you'll start a fire," someone called over across the camp, earning himself a few worn-out chuckles.

The inability to bend my fingers proved to be much more of a nuisance than the pain in my feet. The first year of marching through trenches in the soggy muck gave my feet that constant pain you get in your arms from keeping your hands under cold water for too long. Surprisingly, it's much easier to charge on numb feet than to pull a trigger with frozen hands. The thought made me smile; what I would do to be at home with pains in my hands from my mother shouting at me that my hands better be perfectly clean before I sat at her dinner table. But I needed to forget that. Thinking back and reminiscing were not the things that make life easier out here—it would give me that sharp numbing pain in my chest that knocks the breath clean out of you.

Picking up my bag, I gave it another go, slightly bending my fingers enough to get a good grip. With a small success, I could shove the letter and newspaper clipping to the bottom with all the others. An Easter Rising and executions; how Ireland had changed in two years. All my moaning about the Irish countryside, begging to try the cities where my father's work would be in higher demand, I had never considered myself luckier knowing my parents were tucked away in Tipperary in the aftermath of all the fighting—literal and political. One-week Ireland is condemning the acts of the men who caused the Helena to park herself on the Liffey, bombing the innocent as they slept in their own beds, the next week condemning the British for executing them. I wasn't stupid enough to think my family wouldn't get any slack for their origins or protestant names, but one window being broken with a rock at night wasn't a huge threat considering the fighting and tension blowing up in certain parts.

Ironic, isn't it? All the letters full of their fears and worries for me on the front and now I was scared for them. I must make sure to tell Mother to use my wages to fix it; a broken window would do them no good when winter comes. But, from what they said in their letter, that's even if any Irishman will sell a window to a British one—especially when an Irishman broke the original window. Simon and Will would offer their earnings too, but they know to use mine. They're younger and haven't finished their apprenticeships yet; they won't go home and walk straight into a job. I'm older, I've trained and worked a while; it will be easier for me to have to start my life again with less when this is over.

If it will ever be over…

If I'm still alive when it's over…

October 1916
Egypt. Little Will running around the Nile with a gun that's, more than likely, half his own weight. On second thoughts, it had been over two years since I'd hugged him goodbye. Nothing like a world war to turn a scrawny sixteen-year-old into a rough-and-tough eighteen-year-old. I wonder what it will be like to see them both again. If things will go back to the normal pushing and

shoving, or will they see the faces of their friends suffocating when they fumble too long with a gas mask every time they blink too? Simon was always rather jolly; he might be like the men who sing or tell jokes and stories to cope—but then again, the longer they're here the quieter they get.

Looking up and down the trench at all the men slumped half asleep along the walls, I wonder if I will bump into him— Mother's last letter said Simon had told her all about the poppies blanketing northern France. It made me sad to think he was here but not—looking at the same sky and same landscapes but still miles away from me. Then again, I guess I can't complain. Will is probably feeling a whole lot lonelier on the other side of the fight, the other side of Europe. He probably imagines Simon and I pass each other in the trench, might be in the same camp or may even get the pleasure of eating a meal together. When you grow up looking at the maps, you don't think that countries are half as big as they actually are— Simon may as well be off in Egypt too.

I slouched down a little further on the wall, trying to get comfortable. Looking up to the top of the trench, a red poppy had survived all the men charging and retreating, still fighting the October frost. I have nothing to be moaning about in my next letter, really.

Haven't been hit by a bullet.

Haven't lost a brother.

Much closer to home than Will.

Nothing to complain about… nothing at all…

March 1917

I scanned their letter again, rubbing the bottom corner to make sure there was not another page. Not one mention of Will in this one. Strange, Mother never forgets to tell me how they are, what jokes they made or something they saw that she wouldn't believe.

In her last few letters, if Will didn't stop going on about Egypt, I expect she was going to pack up and set off to go see for herself.

The lack of excitement and half-hope that they were enjoying some of their time there made the letter seem empty and sad. It gave me an uneasy feeling in the pit of my stomach, a wariness as if there was something been kept from me. A whole new kind of numb pain spread in my chest, and from then on, every slim envelope and one-page letter I was handed seemed to knock the breath clean out of my chest.

August 1917

Again, I wrote that they were to use my wages to support themselves. People boycotting my father's shop meant it was hard for them to buy fuel and food; they should have known they could take what they needed without having to ask me. What good is any money to me out here, anyways. It would pass, people back home were fair and friendly, and my parents weren't imperialists or colonialists. The bitterness towards my parents would fade over time when people saw that my middle-aged parents weren't stirring trouble or housing any unionists. A lot of their neighbours were in the same boat—only had sons and all had volunteered to go and fight. Heartbroken mothers would not leave my mother to her own devices when they all needed each other the most.

We moved to Tipperary as tailors there were in few supply, and with my father being in the business as long as he had, his work spoke for itself. He had a lot of customers, a lot of regulars. Bitterness would eventually fade; it was just a case of waiting for the first one to see the fear the Great War put behind mother's eyes passing on the road and put differences aside. Funny; the war protected my parents on two fronts.

April 1918

"As if they couldn't make things any worse!" John plonked down, shoving the newspaper clipping into the hands of the next man. "Conscription! They want to force Irish men to die for them, refuse to acknowledge our culture, heritage, language, even! Read the bottom part... that bit there—see! All of us told to fight to please their government and win their favour for our freedom—we're now being called traitors."

A litany of grumbling and swearing followed it. Any comfort that people wouldn't be cruel to my parents now went out the window. The British government had just made things so much worse for those of us living on the Emerald Isle. The article made its way around the camp and I put my hand out to take it.

"What do you want that for, prod?" John had a cold look in his eyes—not that empty one you get from fighting on the front lines—a hard and unforgiving one. "Haven't you been sent some British newspaper that's lording its success of making us nasty little Irish people cause a fuss again?"

"I was born and raised in Ireland—in Tipp." I lifted my chin and looked him in the eye. I could feel other glares coming from around the camp. "I have the parent's accent, but I've never actually been in England. Sure, look, with all the fighting – I get it. Forget I asked." I leaned back against the tree whose roots I had settled between. Silence followed. I had no interest in making enemies among my camp, among my side of the fight. These were the men that wouldn't be shooting me, and it seemed even they felt we shouldn't be fighting among ourselves.

"Tipperary, eh?" John himself walked over to hand the clipping down to me, not meeting my eyes. Moments like this, back at camps around fires, were where my observing skills grew and I was able to recognise a man on his last nerve, snapping at a comrade before he could think straight and regretting it. "Is it home to the sweetest girl you know?" His pun earned small smiles from the rest of the Irish in the camp.

"Does my mother count?" I got laughs. All the men who had someone to write love letters to, or who had returned from leave with a ring on their finger laughing at all of us writing to our mothers.

"It can be about that too, you know?" someone else piped up. "That song was by an Englishman, ironically. His sweetheart was in Connemara, but he swapped it to Tipp 'cause his gran was from there and it fit better. I like to think of me mam, both me grannies and me fiancé when I hear it."

"Well, there you go," John nodded at me, "a Tipperary song by an Englishman." There were a few moments of quiet before someone started it, men wide awake thinking of home, or half-asleep thinking of tomorrows trek, began to join line by line. Sat on the ground of a French forest looking up at the night sky I thought how this seemed so comforting, yet lonely, before joining in.

"It's a long way to Tipperary,
It's a long way to go,
It's a long way to Tipperary,
To the sweetest girl I know..."

While Joe sang along, eyes closed and drifting into sleep dreaming of home and his mother's cooking, the song carried over to the other camp, who were trading places with them. One group of men pulled back after weeks of fighting, one group going to take their turn at it. He didn't realise that in that very camp, mixed in among the uniforms, lay a man, looking up at the sky, smiling, listening to their singing, thinking of his own home in Tipperary, his mother's homemade bread and his two brothers.

For the first time in a long time, Simon felt as happy as he ever had, looking forward to the day that he would sit down with Joe and Will, not realizing one of them was falling asleep on the other side of the forest.

November 1918

I was expecting the greatest sense of relief when my foot went down on British pavement. Instead, the sharp pain up the back of my legs was my first warning sign of the problems that I had coming to me. It lasted only a moment, then the crowd that had gathered to greet their families returning home swarmed forward and the distraction of watching families reunite pushed it to the back of my mind. The bunting, the children running through the troops looking for their dads, screaming in delight. All the laughter and high-pitched shouting—joy and happiness sounded so strange, so different from the last four years of hopeless mumbling and grunting.

Even though I knew that there was no one here to greet me, I couldn't help but feel giddy at all the excitement. It didn't fade for days to come, pubs and drinks flowing, and if you had a uniform, you were welcomed anywhere as a brother even if no one in the pub knew you. Eventually, I pulled myself away from the celebrations, the singing, the stories and even the dancing; I wanted to be home for Christmas. One long train ride later, I finally stood on the boat bringing me home. The feeling of knowing I was going to see my parents after four long years, going to see my brothers—the two people who would understand everything—was amazing. I even felt happy at the thought of spending my day sewing. I couldn't wait to be shouted at for dragging dirt into the house, or nudging Will's elbow so he spilled tea over the polished table top. Even though I was a grown man, head of the family, I was looking forward to being a bit of a brat for a few weeks.

Things weren't going to be the same, I knew that. There are some things you can't forget, some things that flash up behind your eyelids every time you blink. I didn't expect us to always be cheery, or expect us all to be in one piece, but home was home, and I would try to pretend everything was back to how it was for my family's sake.

Stepping onto Dublin Bay was not like stepping back into London. No one came for any of the soldiers returning. I had told no one to come, so that I could walk up to the front door to see the fire lit, the kettle on and a dinner being kept warm, but had absolutely no one bothered with coming to see any of them? Walking to the train station, the feeling got worse and worse. Strangers gave dirty looks, making a point to look us up and down. Passing a crowd out the front of a shop topped it off with the not so quiet whispers about traitors returning home. I didn't let it slow me down, there was one house that would be happy and welcoming, one house I had being dreaming of, and it was another few hours of a journey away.

Again, no one was waiting for the train when the last few of us got off. Unlike Dublin, we were just ignored here. It was hard to walk along the roads, uneven and full of potholes. I felt like my knees had been filled with acid. The pains in my feet took over for the first time since I spent my first year in the trenches, but the limping got me a pity lift the majority of the way home. There were raised eyebrows and exchanged looks when I thanked them for their kindness with my accent, but they still brought me along with them.

It was fifteen minutes from home where I was dropped off, and they were the most painful fifteen minutes I'd had throughout the war, and that included being shot a few times. I had to stand the entire journey from France to England; I had paced on the boat from Wales to Dublin, but I had sat stationary for over an hour for the first time in a very long time on the back of a cart. I felt like my legs had turned to jelly. Seeing the smoke coming from a certain chimney over the treetops made the shots of pain worth the excruciating walk. I had never cried from happiness before but, limping from the gate to the front door, it was hard to fight back the burning in the back of my throat. I had spent so long thinking I would not walk through this door again and here it was, right in front of me. Time away made me hesitant, though, instead of pushing it open and walking right in I stopped and felt the need to knock, but as I raised my fist the door swung open and there they were.

My father stooped to look out under the door and my mother peeking over his shoulder. I hadn't even hugged my father the day I had left for the war, I hadn't hugged my father since I was a child, but I wrapped my arms around his shoulders without a second thought. To my complete surprise, he hugged me back instead of shoving me off and laughing at me. My mother, on the other hand, barely hugged me, turning away saying I needed a proper dinner.

Following her into the kitchen and sitting down, I noticed she didn't really look at me. My plate was slid across the table as she looked out the window at nothing and she stood staring out the back of the house at nothing with her mug in her hand. It was eerily quiet, like something terrible had happened.

"I'm first home then?" I asked, shoving mashed potatoes into my mouth, waiting for the whack of a newspaper and a reminder of my manners. I had expected at least one of my brothers to be here when I returned. "Simon will be fuming, he loves being number one at everything. I'll be surprised if he hasn't counted how many bullets, he's fired to spite me and Will." She didn't move a muscle, not even a smile, so I looked to my father and, for the first time in my life, I saw tears in his eyes. He took two pieces of paper from the cupboard behind him and left them on the table in front of me. One a telegram and one a letter, both started out with sentences that made me feel like my heart had been ripped out of my chest.

'*Mr. & Mrs. Thompson,*
I deeply regret to inform you...'
'*Mr. & Mrs. Thompson,*
It is my painful duty to inform you that..."

The telegram dated back February 1917, a month before the letter where mother stopped mentioning Will. The letter dated April 1918. I scanned over both of them, feeling the burn in my throat take over. When I thought of coming home, I did not think I would be the only brother to return.

"Simon would be fuming, though, you're right." I had never heard my father's voice break as he spoke before. "Will's telegram came first. Although Simon got a whole letter, so he'd gloat over that I suppose." He tried to let out a little laugh, but it sounded more like a sob. The numb feeling of loss and silence of the house without them, of never really saying a proper goodbye settled over me. I never thought that four years ago was the last time I would see my little brothers when I looked over my shoulder and I waved goodbye as they waited to turn eighteen. That all they would be to me now, little brothers. I never met the war-worn soldiers, and I will never meet the men that should have returned.

After that the dread set in, thinking back to the men gassed— suffocating on air, the men who died from bleeding out of the limbs that had been blown off, the men captured and killed... How had they gone? Was it one of the long and painful ways where you can see them thinking of their lives and loved ones while they wait to go? Not knowing how they went was worse than knowing they would never come home. Will died in Egypt... was he given the quick death of a well-aimed bullet? Simon died in northern France, among the poppies... I knew that one, those flowers flourished during the war because the bombs created an instant fertiliser for them. It was quite ironic how something so delicate and beautiful flourished from something so gruesome. A whistle and a loud boom, gone in an instant... it would have been quick... quick and painless.

As the weeks began to blur by, I got the knack of sewing without really concentrating on it which proved a curse. It was hard not to think about blood-red poppies... not to picture the slow ways I had seen friends and enemies slowly die and have vicious images of my little brothers suffering. The feeling of being a rat trapped in the trenches was the only comparison I could make to now being locked in my own head.

2.

Sitting in my father's small shop, sewing, and sewing would be the activity that supported me for a long time to come. Unlike feeling trapped in the family business and wanting to go see the world before, I looked forward to sitting in the windowless room, learning about sewing machines and practicing stitches. Having something to mindlessly practice and repeat over and over in my head left no room for the nightmares I kept having to repeat in my head all day. I had also not thought of how much better the use of my hands got the longer I worked with my father. Rolling the tape, folding, pinning, stitching and mending—all granted me the gift of closing my fist again. The same could not be said for my feet—standing beside a client or sitting at a table sewing did them no good—I tried bouncing my knee, taking it in turns with either leg. That just gave me cramps, and I could tell it was bugging my father. Tapping my feet quietly on the carpet was no good, after a client gave me a funny look for dancing to no music at my worktable.

After work, I tried going for walks. It took months for me to build a mile up into ten and to be able to walk to work without slowing my father down, or nearly being sick by the time we arrived with the pains I had. The walking gave me relief even from my own home. In the four years I spent yearning to see the chipped, green door, to lie on my own bedsheets and eat in the kitchen—it was all the total opposite. The house was so quiet and empty. I rarely said anything, just agreeing with my father about his comments on the radio news, and my mother only spoke small instructions about groceries or things that needed mending. My room was just my room; they removed the other two beds and their few belongings so I did not have to deal with them. I could never tell them I would have liked to keep Simon's favourite cap or Will's leather gloves, not for my own use but just to have something of them. There were no bodies to bury, so I had no grave to visit.

Even worse, I bit back the anger inside me that wanted to scream at them that they did not have to cut them out of our lives like they had never been there. A few months after the war ended, medals and awards were being dished out. My silent and grieving mother answered the door to the special delivery of a wooden plaque with a golden centre—commemorating Simon for the great work he did as a soldier and the bravery and leadership he displayed. Telling a mother her dead son was going to be promoted to a higher rank and died heroically was no comfort to her, it was hurt and heartbreak. She shoved the plaque into the kitchen cupboard, so every morning I made myself tea before the journey to work I would see it behind the dishes, reminding me that if I had been less competitive with Simon when we were children, and had I not given him this need to best his own brothers, he might not have led the charge across the field where he died. If he was humble and more relaxed, he might have been in the second or third surge, after the bombs had dropped, behind a wall of his fellow soldiers, alive.

What's even worse to do to a grieving mother—send her medals commemorating their service, one more than the other due to rank. Will received one less medal than Simon. I think that was another reason she never hung the plaque. She did not love one of her dead children more than the other, she did not miss one more than the other and, most importantly, she considered either as stupid as the other for running to war for honour, and leaving her with a fraction of her beloved family. Rewarding one more than the other made one look more important, and how could she have more commemorations for one child over the other? Both deserved the same in her eyes—so nothing was displayed or hung out of fairness and love. The look she gave the plaque was one I often saw her giving me out the corner of my eye—it made me realise she did not hate me for surviving when they did not. How could she go on looking at one surviving child, practically crippled, when he resembles the younger two?

The days after I returned from the war became longer and longer, bleeding into what felt like one continuous and painful one. That was my fifth year without a Christmas, and I'd gladly take any of the four Christmas' in France, in oblivion, over this one. There were no birthdays or celebrations of any sorts. No smiles or laughs or dancing to the radio. The war to end all wars impacted the front line and the soldiers away from home for four tedious and cruel years, but it lasted much longer in my house in mourning for the ones who did not come home.

My father decided to split wages evenly with me. He said he was grateful for the support my war pay-packets gave them in 1916 and during the conscription crisis. He also thought as a man of twenty-four with a war behind me and my life ahead of me I should start saving for the future. He even let me take over some loyal clients so I could build my own reputation, as his eyes were acting up and he expected to have to take the backseat on the family business any day soon. He coped considerably better, nudging me with his elbow implying I might want to save for a ring and a ceremony someday.

He never asked for my keep for food, because he wanted to give me a chance at getting ready to have a life—a life I did not want nor plan to go looking for. Despite knowing I would never someday ask any woman to deal with my midnight walks to relieve my feet, sticking my feet as close as I could to the fire to feeling in them again or the moments I could stop moving and fall back into a trance of thinking about the trenches and battlefields, I shoved all of my earnings from war and tailoring into a biscuit tin my mother kept for all the war wages, without realizing that just over a month after I came home, I would end up depending on it heavily...

January 1919

After the post-war meetings, the new borders of Europe were decided, and, despite all their advocating at the meetings, Sinn Féin returned home without Irish independence. The Irish Volunteer Force became the Irish Republican Army using more formidable ways to get independence. Their new methods of advocating and convincing kicked off the Irish War of Independence when they killed two policemen in Tipperary, the safe haven I had been grateful for years ago, now a warzone. The IRA numbers were big in Tipp, so walking to work, getting groceries and even standing in our own front yard became dangerous. Local boys known for being a part of it were disapproved of, but what they fought for was the 800-year-old dream, so no one openly accused or disowned them. My father and I felt the difference. The boys' families seemed to get uncomfortable when they came into the shop, cold to us even. Bit by bit, the more the Irish died in guerilla warfare, they stopped coming at all, and that biscuit tin became very important.

People distancing themselves from the local protestants was difficult for us. My father got on with his life, two children down by appreciating the little things—a father bringing his son into the shop for his first proper coat, getting a man ready for his wedding, chatting about sons with fathers. He started to become like my mother, quiet and solemn—shell-shocked was the word they came up with for soldiers; I saw it in them. My mother's state got even worse. She stayed at home a lot anyway, but her weekly grocery trips lost their chats and the when-and-where of the local ladies tea visits stopped reaching her. But my parents were old and had suffered loss—they were shunned and ignored, but never targeted.

Being a young English man was not as safe, however. Personally, I felt the only reason I didn't get a bullet from a high tree was because boys had been warned by mothers or aunts or grandmothers what it felt like to lose a child, and I was the last of the Thompson boys—I was to be left alone.

I bet when my little brothers signed up to fight for a great cause, to be heroes in the greatest war ever seen in history, they did not realise paying with their lives meant they also saved their oldest brother from getting a hiding. Guilt pressed down on my chest again—the oldest brother, the first child, and I was hiding behind the protection of the two people I should have looked after the most in the world.

3.

By the end of the month, they had arrived. Ex-war soldiers with PTSD issues and a lot of pent-up anger, taking full advantage of their position and their weapons. In my part of Tipperary, they mainly shot civilians from behind. They earned the title *Black and Tans,* and if you were unfortunate enough to have an accent like theirs, you were presumed as guilty for their bullets as they were. My father and I refused to let mother go to town anymore. Being as rural as we were, she had a few roads and fields to walk, a few cousins still wrote to her but the isolation with a bereaved father and a shell-shocked son started to get to her. I hated to see it, but she was alive, and she never had to know the feeling of being shot nor gotten a look from the wife of an injured civilian. I never knew what to say to her anymore.

The summer came and it was the warmest I could remember. But that was when it hit me again. Winter in a house where there were empty seats and beds took a while to get used to. When summer came and traditions like swimming in the rivers and going out drinking were gone too, it was like getting hit with the news all over again. You think you're used to it; you've accepted they're gone and bam. Another tradition to do alone, another song that was one's favourite. Sweets that the youngest loved, but you could only get in the summer months. The loneliness never left, and without realizing it, my father and I became just like my mother. Empty, quiet and solemn: With that, the year went by in a blink—an entire year of my life that I cannot remember. That is how cruel the mind can be, the darkest and most gruesome details of war engraved in my brain, things I can never forget. A year at home, warm and fed just a blur. Or maybe it was a kindness not to remember a year of content and feeling safe— instead of being hit again with the blood and casualties of Civil War, I was able to shut it all out." Spring 1920 is the first thing that comes to my mind after my return home. My father brought home a bunch of flowers for my mother after the weekly messages. She was panicking—he had been gone longer than needed, and I was pacing around the front yard telling myself I would go looking for him on the hour when he walked through the gate. At the time, I was annoyed at him when I heard the gate and turned to give him a dirty look—he could have told me he wanted to buy her flowers from the shop at the other side of the town and add some of her favourites to it from a few fields away. But looking at him I couldn't help but laugh. With four bags, he had no hands to carry them, so he shoved the ones he bought into his shirt—blue and purple and yellow sticking out the top of his shirt at his throat and shoved the wild ones into his socks—pink and red. I couldn't decide if he looked like an over-achieving clown or the friendliest scarecrow I had ever seen. He winked at me, handing me the bags and began to assemble them all. Then I got a better view of his own additions. Poppies.

"Where in the name of God –"

My mother's shrill shouting stopped when she saw the flowers.

"It's been five years since we celebrated our wedding anniversary, Eliza." My father held out the flowers. "Seeing as the fighting has come to our doorstep, I have decided I am not going to look at the half empty glass anymore. Our neighbours are burying their husbands and sons. We have lost two of the three people we loved more than anything, but one of them came home. I have not been shot at yet. Our house has not been raided or burned down by either side of the fight yet. We have done alright so far. So, we should enjoy the son that came home and the house of memories that we have and the freedom to move without aggravating a wound. Happy Anniversary, my darling." He kissed her on the head. I wondered what had gotten into him to do that—to pick himself back up.

My mother smiled down at her flowers and brought them in to put them in water. From then on, my father surprised her once a month, randomly with flowers, chocolates, sweets or little bits of jewellery. I might not have had their newfound enthusiasm, but I got to look at my parents come back to life and enjoy it. By the end of the summer, the wooden plaque commemorating Simon Thompson's bravery and sacrifice was hanging on the kitchen wall, and beside it was a homemade one for William Thompson.

After walking home from the local post office to apply to work on the extension of a local railway track, I met my angry mother on the doorstep.

"What are these?" She shoved three medals into my face.

"War medals." I snapped them to return them to their box under my bed. "Why were you looking in there?"

"I was spring cleaning, and I know how you just shove things away, so I went through your clothes, got rid of anything town or worn—as a tailor's son you should be ashamed, you can easily make yourself new ones—and I thought it was a shoe box, so I opened it. When did you get these?"

"One in 1917 for 1914, one in 1919 for 1917 and one in 1919 for all four years of service. I'm sorry you had to look at them." I dropped them in the box and shoved it under my bed.

"Why are you sorry?"

"Because... I just am." I'm sorry I lived, and they didn't. I'm sorry you only have me. I'm sorry I didn't die instead of them.

"They got some too." She crossed the hall to her room and came back with five medals. Sitting on my bed, she patted the space beside her. Even sitting down, she didn't reach my shoulder. "Three for Simon, and two for Will." She lay them out perfectly, straightening the ribbons across our laps. "I put them away. But over the summer I've been thinking your father was right—we should be happy for what we have. You should not have hidden them from me, Joe, I would have been happy to see them."

I thought on how I should explain it to her—what I should say without upsetting her?

"Well mother, I'm not happy to see them." My eyes filled with tears. She was my mother; she knew me the best and she knew what I was fighting back. Instead of looking at me and making me embarrassed, she held my hand.

"Can I have them so? For my collection of all my son's bravery?" I nodded and reached down for the box, handing it to her. Without saying anything, my mother knew what I was admitting—when it comes to those years, I just can't. Can't talk about it, can't explain it, can't see the bright side. And I don't think I will ever want to. The next morning when I got up, the plaques were gone from the kitchen. I felt too guilty to ask, but weeks later I was relieved to catch a glimpse of them in their room above my mother's old dresser: eight medals all shining and displayed, and one blurry black and white photo of three young boys with their arms wrapped around each other's shoulders.

That autumn, I was hired for the railroad and joined countless other men in digging and laying. Not many spoke to me after they heard my 'prod name', but they did not make it difficult on me either. I was with them working when there was fighting going on and with time, I think they accepted my innocence without me once arguing or fighting with any of them. Given time everyone was reasonable—people only reacted harshly out of sudden feelings, in the moment stuff. Keeping quiet and biding time-built bridges with my colleagues and neighbours and that was something I carried with me for the rest of my life. People just need time.

After one of the longest shifts I had done on the site, I joined everyone in rolling my shoulders and neck from being stooped over. I could never do that at home. The money took pressure off my parents budgeting our combined savings, and it made me happy to see them treating each other to new shawls and shirts. Passing through the village half of the group split into the pub and half into Hackett's for sweets and cold drinks. I didn't mind the work in the summer going there and leaving while its sunny especially now that there was a ceasefire—it was enjoyable.

A high-pitched shriek nearly had me jumping out of my skin. Looking back at the village, a drunk had a barmaid caught by the elbow.

"I don't care who you are or what you think you're entitled to, but a bill is a bill." She couldn't be more than five-feet-tall, shouting up at a man twice her size and drunk.

"I fought for this country, pet." He leaned down to snarl in her face. I started making my way back. "I fought against the black and tans, took out a few of them, too. The owner knows

33

that, and I drink for free here."

"I couldn't careless! He lets you drink because of your threats—he's scared of you. A drunk like you couldn't do anything worth being afraid for. I'm the only one here that has it in me to say it! Now pay or piss off." I'm sad to say he had slapped her before I got to him, but it worked in my favour. The force knocked her to the ground, out of his grip and I could pin him without hurting her.

"No need to hurt a girl like that." He spat over his shoulder at me.

"Oh look, the local prod. Heard about you, Thompson, you seem a bit too good to be true. Come on, let's see what the war taught ya." I used his weight to gain momentum, hopping him off the wall again.

"What's the problem here, gentlemen." Before I could open my mouth to the copper, the barmaid was on her feet.

"That alcoholic threatened the owner of this pub. I called him out for not paying his bill and he dragged me out here and hit me. See." She walked right up to him, stood on her tiptoes and pointed to her cheek were the handprint was so big on her little face. It was mainly just the palm and one ring he wore leaving a mark.

"I see." The copper looked at me. "And you stepped in to help?" I nodded.

"Joe Thompson, sir." He raised an eyebrow at the surname.

"Ah, Thompson. You must be bang out of order to get him riled up and pinning you to the wall, ey Tommy? You can think on your attitude in the station cell tonight." He glanced down at the barmaid. "You're fair, pet, that will bruise. Get it looked at." He cuffed Tommy and dragged the shouting, slurring drunk off with him. The barmaid turned to look at me. He was right—she

34

needed to make sure he didn't break anything because her face was already a funny colour.

"I had that under control, but thanks." She folded her arms and stuck her pointy chin in the air.

"Of course, you did." I looked at my boots to hide my laughter, I didn't want to upset her even more.

"You all right, Cáit?" The pub owner's head stuck out the back door.

"I am, no thanks to you!" She had a whole lot of attitude, and scolded the middle-aged man as if she was his mother. "Mr Thompson is the reason I only got a slap, and nothing worse." He nodded sadly and glanced up at me.

"A pint on the house whenever you like as a thanks for helping her–"

"For feck's sake, stop being the big man giving out drink left, right and centre! Look what happened the last time." She pointed in the direction Tommy was dragged off. He shut the door quickly behind him, escaping another scolding.

"Come on," I nodded towards the road, "I know where the doctor lives. I'll walk you. It's after ten, so it's not safe or right to let you walk alone, please don't argue with me on it." I cut her off before she started. She nodded and ran inside for her shawl and purse. Her shawl had bright white and yellow daisies all over it and nearly completely covered her.

"Are we walking in awkward silence, or?" She raised an eyebrow at me.

"Forgive me, I forgot my manners. Joe Thompson, tailor and railway-worker." She shook my hand. "And you're Cáit?"

"Mary-Kate, You make clothes and build railways?"

"A man of many talents." I stuck my nose in the air and then caught myself by surprise. I hadn't tried to get a smile out of anyone in years. She snorted.

"Uh-huh. What part of England are you from?" She sure didn't tip toe around the elephant in the room.

"I was born here, but my parents are from Kent. I got the accent from them." She nodded.

"And you're a war veteran? That isn't an alcoholic?" It was my turn to nod. "Many talents indeed."

"I have two grieving and old parents to support. I have no time to drown my sorrows yet."

"Yet? So, when they go you will. Goodness me, what a waste of all that talent." I bit the inside of my cheek, we seemed to be in battle of who would get the first laugh. "Won't please me nor give me the win, no?"

"Absolutely not."

"You've certainly forgotten your manners this evening."

I stole a glance at her. She was only up to my elbow, tiny frame and all. Red hair and big green eyes—now with a green cheek to match them. Looking down, I could see her worn hands from cleaning in the pub and they were slightly trembling. She can make all the banter she wants; she still got a fright.

"It's rude to stare." I looked ahead. "You're very jumpy, ain't you?"

"You seem to be quite the force to be reckoned with. I wouldn't dare cross you." I straightened my back like a soldier marching next to her.

"*Finally,* a man that understands that behaving to my standards is all I require for a nice conversation." She won. I laughed out loud and looked back down at her.

"Ah, so men are the problem?"

She nodded profusely. "Absolutely. And don't talk like that, you sound like my mother."

We arrived at the doctor's door, and he answered straight away. Not even five minutes later, she had a numbing cream and painkillers for the week until it healed. I was waiting to walk her back to the pub when she came out the door and pointed up at me.

"He walks with a little bit of a limp and his neck bothers him. He's a tailor and a railway worker it's probably from stooping over a table or a hole somewhere. Not to mention he's bigger than a door frame and probably has to duck everywhere he goes." I stared down at her mouth agape. "You'll catch flies." She stood on her tiptoes and her little hand pushed my chin up.

"Bad feet from the trenches, lad?" I nodded at the doctor. "Well, let's not have a bad back to go with that." He gave me muscle cream and a leaflet on stretching exercises. "Be sure to do them."

"I'll make sure he will." Mary-Kate shoved me out the door and snapped it shut behind us.

"You told on me!" I opened the gate for her.

"Just something I noticed." She shrugged.

"And may I ask how will you be checking I do my exercises?"

"Well, you struggled to stop staring at me on our walk here – and you're doing it again." I looked away. "So, I will make sure you use your cream and have done your exercises—'cause I can spot lies a mile off – when you take me for a drink after my shift tomorrow night. If you are courting someone, I will get them to check."

"You're telling me I'm going to ask you out?"

"You seem shy, I'm being supportive and giving you that little push." She smiled up at me. "So, will I see you tomorrow at ten thirty, or will you tell me where your girlfriend lives, so I can tell on you again?" I smiled to myself. She was small, but bloody mighty.

"I will see you tomorrow. But I am considered the local 'proddie'–"

"Yes, yes, I know. I don't need the chivalrous warning about the implications of taking me on a date. But a pub full of Irish men, some of whom are my cousins, sat there staring while Tommy dragged me outside, and you came to help and made sure I went to the doctor. I see a good kind man, not a British or Irish one."

Mary-Kate went back to finish her shift insisting she needed to shame all the men who sat there while she was dragged out by her hair. I went home with a strange giddy feeling in my stomach. I had given up on planning a future or going looking for a wife or family after the war. I certainly did not expect it after the last three years of fighting. But it seemed she had made up her mind, and although she didn't know where I lived, I was scared to think of the implications of not showing up. The image of a tiny Irish woman waiting outside the railway site to chase me down appeared in my mind like one of those comics in the papers and I chuckled. I wouldn't put it past her.

The next morning my mother got the shock of her life when I told her why I got up early before work.

"I need to go into town." Porridge was too hot for a June summer, but it would last me longer than toast considering I was walking half an hour in the opposite direction of my job.

"For what? Your clothes are all ok, and I just got this week's messages."

"Flowers."

"Flowers?" Both my parents looked at me like I was gone insane.

"Yeah." I scraped the bowl clean. "I know it's late notice, but any chance you'd iron my good shirt, mother?" She nodded. "Do they do bunches of daisies? Or are they too common in the fields?" I looked at my father.

"They um, they do, son." I washed out my bowl and left it beside the sink.

"Grand, I'll be back after work, can you keep them alive until tonight?" My mother nodded, still at a loss for words. I went into the hall and shoved my shoes on.

"Be back on time to wash up—no point in a clean shirt if you stink." My father and mother stared out the kitchen door at me. I gave them a smile and a thumbs up which just freaked them out.

"Joe, what in the name of God are you up to?" my mother whispered in shock.

"Barmaid in the village beside the site—Mary-Kate. Stepped in when a drunk smacked her, walked her to the doctor to get pain killers and she told me I was going asking her on a date. Back in a bit, bye." I shut the door before I was dragged back into the kitchen for more questions, smiling at the looks on their faces when I said 'date'. 1921 was the first year in six years that I felt genuinely happy, all thanks to a tiny barmaid wrapped in daisies.

4.

"Plans for the evening?" One of the lads from the site looked me up and down as I passed Hackett's, flowers tucked under my arm.

"Yeah"

"Who's the unlucky girl?" They all laughed. I smiled, straightening my collar.

"Mary-Kate." They laughed even louder.

"Best of luck lad, she turns everyone down. If you bug her, she will say yes, get you to come in at the busiest hour and make an eejit out of ya in front of the whole pub!"

"Oh, I've already gotten the date—she arranged it." I smiled at them and marched inside. The pub was considerably full, but then again it was Friday night.

"She's upstairs changing and doing her hair with the wife; she'll be down soon. Never a minute late." I nodded to the pub owner, Murphy, and sat down at an empty booth right up the back. I left the daisies down on the table and fidgeted with my collar again. My parents had gotten over the surprise by the time I came back from work and were in full swing trying to do me up. I agreed to some of my father's cologne as I was walking to the date, but I drew the line at gelling my hair back. I can make an effort, but I sure as hell wasn't making myself into something I am not.

"Good—you're early." Mary-Kate dropped down into the seat opposite me. "I hate tardiness, so inconsiderate. Well, you've scrubbed up." I could only stare at her. Her hair was now pinned to the back of her head, and she wore a purple dress, making her eyes look even more green, if it was possible. Stuck for what to say, I slid the daisies across the table.

"Oh, my favourite! Lucky guess." She smirked at me.

"I didn't guess." I sat up proudly. "You had daisies on your shawl yesterday. Patterned material is more expensive than plain, you or someone in your family spent that extra money because you like daisies. I notice things, too." I actually made her blush under her bruises. She caught my successful smile.

"Well, don't get too confident, I've worked here for years, I'm used to flirty men and their compliments. Making me blush won't be a regular occurrence."

"Challenge accepted." I nodded. "Drink?"

I sat there with Mary-Kate for the whole night, right up to closing time and after while Murphy cleaned up. I learned everything I could about her: two older brothers, shifts in the pub, Catholic, feisty, hard-working and the most amazing person I had ever met.

I was not as good as talking as she was. I could tell her facts but stories about my childhood all involved my brothers and the last six years I could not put into words, but she noticed, and she changed the subject for me. Behind the fire in her eyes, she was kind and compassionate and I had no idea what she was doing on a date with me.

I left that night with the promise to see her next Friday night and that I would take her to town for lunch on Saturday. As happy and as hopeful as I was, I knew it would fizzle out. I wake up in the middle of the night screaming, I already have health conditions that will worsen with age, and I cannot even speak about the brothers I have lost years later because I cannot cope with it. But I sure do plan on enjoying having her in my life while it lasts. As sappy as it sounded, she made me feel alive again.

I could see light coming from the kitchen opening my front door—my mother was waiting for an account of the night and, most importantly, the girl. I basically repeated the entire evening's conversation to her, but it was still not enough, and my mother was annoyed I did not have a kiss on the cheek to tell her about.

I spent my week at work looking forward to the weekend. It was the longest week of my life, but as I walked through the pub door with another bunch of daisies, it felt like it had gone so quickly, and I had no time to think. This week, Mary-Kate wore a pale, blue dress—to match my eyes, she said. Despite the difference in lives and already knowing the basics about each other, we had plenty to talk about and again, stayed past the opening hours. I had been scolded by my mother for not walking her home, but she had told me she worked here for years and I assumed she lived close-by. She turned down my offer as her younger brother walked her home from work every night, and it would be improper for me to be alone with her, in the dark for a six-mile walk in the opposite direction to where I needed to go— a doctor visit was different. Six miles away, to and from every day, no wonder she was so slim.

Lunch in town, the next day was nice; mid-day warmth in the sun and a cool breeze, we ate in the park. Not at all to my surprise, I caught a glimpse of my parents taking a stroll past the park half-way through our lunch date, and back again, trying to get a glimpse of her face seeing as our backs were turned to them. It was too soon to introduce her, but it made me wonder about her family.

"Shouldn't your father have escorted you to meet me by now?" The tradition was that the father accompanied the daughter on all dates to ensure they were proper and to see if the man was suited and approved of.

"My father raised me; he knows I'm capable of looking after myself." I don't think she realised she touched her bruised cheek as she said it. It seemed to be a sore reminder she was not entirely invincible. "Besides our first two dates, Murphy was there, and both my brothers are in town getting the messages today, so they brought me to and from town. If we were eating inside, they would eat in the same café, but we're in broad daylight. Besides, I've told them all you're a gentle and soft soul." I choked on my orange juice. "Not like you're a pushover or anything, just kind but tough 'cause of the war, and defending me so you've already won them over," she stuttered in her rush to save my ego.

"It's fine." I waved off her compliments. "You just always catch me by surprise, that's all." Sitting in the sun with her made it harder to think than usual. Her hair showed up redder, her light freckles stood out more and her eyes glimmered in the sunlight.

"Oh shoot, have I gotten some jam on my face?" she reached up to dab around her mouth with her handkerchief, a daisy had been embroidered on one corner, getting self-conscious at me analysing her face.

"No, Mary-Kate." I pulled her hand away from her face. "You're just so bloody beautiful." Another blush. "I thought they were hard to come by?" I playfully nudged her, teasing her with my small victory.

"Well, yes, it's just... you know." She looked down, fidgeting with her sunhat on her lap.

"Just what?"

"Punters and alcoholics say I'm pretty and pass the most disgusting remarks about me when I'm working, so I've heard all the flirty stuff and all the gross stuff too, but I've never gotten an actual compliment before."

"Well, for my sake I'm glad for it, but you must have only ever met absolute idiots before." She smiled and blushed again. Two in the space of five minutes—I was on a roll.

"Usually, I've offended or put any man I've met off before they consider me. That's why my family aren't being fussy. They're glad you put up with my temper." I watched her getting all uncomfortable and embarrassed admitting something that made her vulnerable to me.

"That fire of yours keeps me on my toes, and to be honest keeps me thinking what to say to try and catch you off guard. What I can say to keep you interested in me. And being really honest, my mind is not the nicest place after the war. There are lots of things I saw that I can't forget; things I picture happening to my brothers that haunt me every living minute of my day. But I forget that stuff on our dates, Mary-Kate." She scoffed, ducking her head to hide another blush.

"This is our third date, Joseph." She always uses my full name. "Don't be all silly."

"I'm not," I defended myself, "I know how quick life can be over and I am simply seizing every moment I get with you. You should know, I like you very much Mary-Kate." Forgetting her pride, she looked right at me, cheeks as red as the roses I had given her today.

"Well, I guess I don't feel so self-conscious with you. And I like you very much too, Joseph." I left that date with enough confidence to give her a kiss on the cheek.

"Well, you could have invited her for a walk when you saw me trying to look." I was getting a scolding.

"We were still eating, mother." I slurped my tea. *Whack!* Tea towel to the back of the head.

"Manners, Joe! Well, you had been there an hour before we left home. What took you so long to eat?"

"Eliza, it was a picnic—more a little buffet than a meal."

"*Hmph.*" I could not believe how much my mother had come back to life since the summer. I never thought I'd be happier to be on the receiving end of one of her rants again; I couldn't help but smile into my dinner.

"She practically lives on the other side of the county." My father reminded me of my guilt for inviting her to lunch so far away from her, but I had blurted it out before I had thought.

"They got a lift on a cart headed up county to relatives, so it wasn't so bad, but I know. " I cut off my father's glare before it turned into a reminder of my manners. "I won't make that mistake again; I'm even going to a Céilí in her local village."

"A what?"

"It's a dance. They take the wooden doors off the closest pubs, stables and houses lay them down on the crossroads because it's the flattest and largest piece of the road. They play traditional music and Irish dance in shoes that make loud noises, like tap shoes."

"And what happens when you're standing to the side watching some lad spin your date around the uh, dance floor, you don't know the steps, and someone asks you why?"

"I've kept myself out of trouble so far," I shrugged. "Besides, Mary-Kate is local, I'm not hiding behind her, but she is a force to be reckoned with. I doubt I would have time to react if anything even happened before she'd dish out a scolding."

"The Irish fought to preserve their culture—the music, the language and the dancing. I have a bad feeling about what the reaction will be to a British bystander." So, my father had completely turned his opinion around on courting Mary-Kate.

"Ok, so you say that now, and I—a non-political man—refuse to go with her on political reasons in fear of my own safety. Then, in a few weeks I look to introduce her, and she's not allowed to come by her father's political grounds. I'm not starting a tit for tat fight with anyone. I will act and treat people the same way I expect to be treated myself. Anyone starts anything, it's their problem."

I felt bad for a few days going against my parents—being the only child left I felt I should keep them as happy as I could, but I had to be my own man too. All of that guilt vanished the night of the Céilí. Mary-Kate flew across that dance floor, hair in full swing under the autumn moon and not a second thought of what anyone there thought of her protestant, British date. She even dragged me up for a slower waltz, insisting I could not come to a dance and stand on the side the entire night. That was the first time I really felt it—the nerves and the fear that you get when you first stand close to someone you really like. I thought about everything and nothing at once—her tiny hands that were no bigger than the palm of my hands, how she kept her head tipped back to look up at me the whole dance and how right it felt to just have her in my arms. That was the actual moment I fully forgot about the war, my injuries or anyone I had lost, and I seriously began to consider a lifetime of that feeling.

I persisted in meeting Mary-Kate throughout the winter of 1921, and even became acquainted with her younger brothers. The locals in Murphy's pub got used to me being there either waiting for Mary-Kate to finish her shift or whisking her away a little before it was technically over. It really was like something from one of those old English books, my mother loved so dearly, but not all fairy tales last, and December brought the first incident in our relationship that made me consider breaking things off for her sake.

The Anglo-Irish treaty had been signed and there was outrage. At the time, I was twenty-five years-old and I considered my patience to be a curse the first weekend after the treaty had been signed that I was walking home from a few drinks with Mary-Kate. In all fairness, the four young men kept quiet as a mouse as I passed them, and even when they walked up behind me. And their planning tactics were impeccable—a bend in the road where a tree shielded us from anyone taking a shortcut home through the fields and no houses nearby to hear me getting jumped. I tried to spite them by keeping my mouth shut but my silence only drove them further.

I was unable to walk with the pain from my old injuries flaring in the cold and the multiple new ones, and it was a few hours later some stragglers leaving the pub after last call found me. I expected to be left, but to my surprise I was picked up. I recognised some of the faces from Murphy's before I passed out from the pain in my ribs.

That beating nearly drove my mother back into her shock. When I came to the next day, she was an unnatural grey colour and my father looked furious.

"I knew it was too good to be true," he was barely whispering, trying to keep himself calm for my mother. "Hanging around an Irish pub and going to Irish dances was going to backfire."

"We're in the middle of Ireland—where else do you suggest I drink?"

"Don't get smart. Did you know you'd been stabbed in the leg? If you had not been found, you could have bled to de–"

"Found by Irish men, right? Don't tar them all with the one brush father. It's a touch hypocritical considering you chose to live here and don't want to be treated like an imperialist or a colonialist."

"They stayed, you know," my mother chimed in, she still had a distant disconnected look in her eyes, but she was contributing at least. "Those young men who brought you home fetched a doctor and stayed outside all night to be sure you'd wake up alright."

"Outside?" I looked up to my father. He just scoffed. But before he could pass another snide comment, a loud demanding voice came from the front.

"And why can't I go in? Of all of us out here I should get to see him!... Who cares what his father thinks, I'm not exactly a big threat." Being so light, her stamping through the front door and into my room couldn't be heard and she simply appeared in the doorway—face red from the cold, bits of snow in her hair, hands on her hips and a very angry look on her face. I could imagine she would feel self-conscious later, but she looked bloody amazing to me. She stared down at me for a few minutes taking in my injuries—broken ribs, black eyes, a stab wound— and genuinely looked lost for words. With my mother beside my bed, I knew this was the time I could get away with holding my good arm out to her for her to fling herself into a hug without it being deemed improper.

"Well, it seems I'll have to start walking you home." She straightened out her skirt and folder her arms. She made my mother smile.

"Listen, Mary-Kate." I sat up slowly wanting to be as proper as I could explaining my decision to her.

"No!" she cut me off. "You are not breaking up with me, we will continue courting – in fact, I would like you to meet my parents at Sunday dinner next weekend, if you're up for the journey. This is not getting to you, you are not allowed to make rash decisions and therefore I will be making them for you." Even when I was injured, she was still giving orders to me.

"Well, that's you told." My mother smiled down at me and stood up grabbing her in a hug. Mary-Kate was not expecting it and glanced at me in panic before relaxing. Then, my unpredictable and brave Irish girl turned to my father, cleared her throat and in the politest tone she could muster, extended her hand.

"Hello, Mr. Thompson." I looked pleadingly at my father; he was rarely ever angry, but when he was, he was completely unpredictable. For the first time in my life, I saw his anger simply melt away as he chuckled and grabbed her hand.

"Hello, Miss Ryan. I must say it's a pleasure to see my son being put in his place and left speechless. Good to know there's a woman out there who is willing to think for him, but I do warn you, you may end up doing it a lot more than you expect." For a second, my happiness made the pain fade as my parents silently gave me their blessing and their approval for Mary-Kate.

"He's right, pet, with Thompson men it truly is a full-time job." Relaxing at my mother's joke, Mary-Kate sat down on the edge of my bed and wrapped her too-little hand around my big one. Feeling guilty for his temper, my father ducked out of the room to invite my friends in out of the cold for tea and a thank-you.

"I'm so glad to finally meet your little daisy." My mother winked at me, hanging me out to dry.

"Ahem, his daisy?" One eyebrow shot up – pending the next piece of information I would be found guilty or innocent.

"Well, we nicknamed you that because of all the daisies he buys you—I see you're fond of them." I hadn't realised in all the

49

panicking that she had a daisy print dress under her jumper.

"I think of you more as an Irish rose," I piped up, acting all poetic and romantic. "Gorgeous in every way, but as sharp and as dangerous as the thorns on the stem."

"Joe, that is hardly flattering—"

"No, it's sweet. I like how you've noticed how much I love daisies." Mary-Kate smiled at me, but there was a glint in her eye. Oh dear. "You can tell anyone I'm your daisy anytime, Joseph. You're my Galway girl." She winked down at me.

"Excuse me?" she looked to my mother and back at me.

"Well, isn't it obvious?" We shook our heads, unfamiliar with the pun. "Joseph," she leaned closer to me to state the obvious, "your hair is black, and your eyes are blue." Laughter rang in from the kitchen seeing as all doors were open and the cottage was small. My mother laughed so hard she cried, and I got the biggest gloating smirk.

"Thank you, Mary-Kate. I compared you to a rose and the entire pub will now be calling me Galway girl."

"Not just the pub, son!" My father's jeer came out from the kitchen and the laughter filled the house again.

5.

With the doctor and a few lads vouching for me, the foreman allowed me to continue on the railway site doing light work. It was coming to the end of the project, so I only had another few weeks of income left from it, but it all counted in the end. Despite both myself and my mother objecting, my father began to organise to reopen the shop in the new year, insisting he was going cracked doing small bits here and there at the house.

The fighting had ended, yes, but we were aware we were living in an unhappy Free State. My mother was able to return to doing her own messages and, although it hurt like hell with every breath, it seemed my injuries brought a silver lining for her. The attack on me was seen as either unnecessary or asking for unwanted trouble. Most families around felt that we were quiet and took our silence on politics as a good thing, the rest of them felt that as an ex-war soldier I could have given just as good as a beating as I got—but I had chosen not to. I tried not to let the fact that, with my legs and my feet constantly burning, that was not true hurt my pride too much. Christmas also seemed to keep people happier as they looked back towards their own families instead of at ours. Within two weeks of popping into town getting the messages, my mother had a tea booked with the neighbours.

Apart from the few who felt enough at ease to tease me about my new nickname, I was getting nods and salutes from my colleagues and fellow drinkers. But, a week into the new year, Mary-Kate stood beside me on her doorstep on a Sunday evening, when she dropped her bombshell—she hadn't been totally honest with her family.

"You've no reason to be nervous." Her accent was thicker—she was nervous. The irony.

"I have two jobs now that the shop is back, and people around don't seem to mind me, I should do okay at getting on with them." Mary-Kate swallowed while she straightened my collar.

"Well, just so ya know—the whole 'you-being-British' thing hasn't really come up."

"Excuse me?"

"I know, I know. It's mean I said nothing until you were here, but I have no idea how Dad will react to a–"

"An Englishman?" she kept her head down unnecessarily, pulling at her cardigan sleeves.

"A protestant, Joseph." Oh. It never even dawned on me the difference in religions would cause issues with her family. I had spent the last month just being so happy on our dates or worrying about rivalry between our two nations; I had not stopped to even realise we were two different religions. I wasn't a devout mass goer, I didn't feel I needed to be front row every Sunday, and being honest, it was hard to believe in a 'God' after the war. Unfortunately, before another word could be said, the door swung open and Mary-Kates's mother smiled up at me.

"Ah ye're back from the pub lunch. Come in, Joseph, come in. We won't get to know you on the doorstep." Somehow, she was even smaller than Mary-Kate, but twice the strength. I barely had any time to duck when she pulled me by the wrist through the cottage door. In the kitchen, her two brothers and father occupied the chairs by the stove.

"Joseph's here," Mrs. Ryan unnecessarily announced. Mary-Kate's brothers nodded, and her father stood up and shook my hand.

"Nice to meet you, lad, sit down there at the end of the table."

"Will you have tea? Ah sure, of course you will." Mrs. Ryan flew from cupboard to cupboard. Mary-Kate sat beside me and gave me an apologetic smile. This would probably be one of the few times in our lives she would admit she was slightly wrong.

"Now, your courting my daughter hasn't been so traditional," Mr. Ryan leaned forward onto the table, "I tried my best with her after she turned seventeen, but she scared most of them off. I figured, when I heard about you and once my boys had seen ya around, with Murphy watching, I would let it happen because she decided for herself. And, if you haven't already discovered, no one tells Mary-Kate what to do."

"You could say that again," her brother, John, muttered into his cup, getting a nervous laugh out of me. She kicked me under the table. I knew I should say something and casually bring up the elephant in the room, but I didn't know where to begin.

"You're very quiet lad, but I heard that. I went into Murphy's today and asked about ya, I'll admit. All good things though. Two jobs, hard-working and the kindest gentleman in the south."

"Thank you, sir." No one noticed.

"Feck it, Mary-Kate, how did you get him?"

"One more time Johnny and I swear–"

"Enough!" Mrs. Ryan somehow managed to keep her two sons and Mary-Kate in check.

"Tell us more about you, Joseph, your family and stuff we've only heard a small bit about you. The lads at the pub seemed to think I should get most of my information directly out of you." He chuckled as all eyes turned to me. I swallowed and smiled at Mrs. Ryan. Of course, they were discreet—all the gossiping in the world, but everyone decided to let Mary-Kate's family find out I was 'the enemy' at their kitchen table.

"Joseph Thompson, sir." I nodded down at her father and watched as four of the five faces looking at me dropped. "Best to get this out of the way. Born in Carlow, served in the great war. Working in my father's tailoring shop, and I will take over one day. I've been in England twice in my life—the way to the front line and the way back." You could hear a pin drop. Mr. Ryan looked down into his mug of tea so I could no longer gauge his face. John and Anthony stared right at me while Mrs. Ryan gave her daughter an appalled look.

"Mary-Kate…"

"I know, Mother, okay? It's just if I said anything you wouldn't even let him in to meet him and then it wouldn't be proper courting, and I'm sick of being reminded of it around the village. *'Your father hasn't accompanied you', 'You're not doing it proper', 'People were happy for ya but are staring to talk, Cáit'.* But I knew if ye met him you'd all see he's really quiet and nice – how could I do that if ye left him on the doorstep. At least try to get to know him."

"Fair enough." I was relieved he wasn't shouting at either of us to get out. "But I would have been, and I still am right about this not working."

"Dad, please listen–"

"No. Thompson is a protestant name, he is from another religion; you would never be able to marry him in a way that any of us or the parish would accept, and I'll be damned if you convert to being a prod for him."

"John senior, your language." Mrs. Ryan's voice was still very quiet.

"Come on now, Eileen. How did she think this would work? And ya let me into the pub asking about him—I knew Murphy looked shifty, you should not have asked him to keep your secrets. Half the parish will think I'm mad, they probably have since you first met. And he fought in that bloody war for them. You know they're all seen as traitors to this country. There's more than one issue here, Cáit."

"I would convert." I said it quietly, hoping he has stopped talking and wasn't getting the breath for more. Her brothers and Mrs. Ryan heard me; now all three wore the same surprised face.

"What?" Mary-Kate's voice was barely a whisper.

"And let's say you had children one day, how—what did you say, Thompson?"

"I would convert to Catholicism for her. There is no age limit on a Christening, right?" They all nodded. "So when I propose, I will convert and have a catholic church wedding. Our children would be raised catholic and be seen as Irish when they went to their parish schools and church every Sunday of their lives."

"But, Joseph, your religion."

"Mary-Kate, please. I do not want to talk about it too much, but I served for four years as a soldier. I left my two brothers behind on those battlefields. I saw horrific… things. Religion is just something difficult now. But, for you, I would convert, because I'll be damned if I let the fact that we were born into different versions of one book stop me marrying you. Sure, who knows—there might be something in ye're version of the book that makes me believe; the Irish lads were always so attached to their medallions." I finished my tea and let it set in.

"I don't like this at all. If you've such a free and practically pagan view on God and mass, so happy to jump ship so quickly, what impression would you make on my grandchildren?" Mr. Ryan stared right down at me.

"Well, I think having a father who would work as many jobs

as he could and do anything for them would be a grand example for children. I'm sure Mary-Kate would set an excellent example." He said nothing.

"I like him, Da." John glanced at his father and back to me.

"I'm not sure," Anthony chimed in, "he seems to have thought about a life with Mary-Kate, I can't decide if he's brave or stupid. But I'm happy to give him time to see which." Mrs. Ryan gave me a small smile around her son's shoulder.

"We'll see." Well, it was a start from the hard no we had gotten five minutes ago.

"Well." I stood. "I have work early tomorrow, and I don't want to overstay my welcome. It was nice to properly meet you all." I walked out the kitchen without waiting for a response or the embarrassment of not getting one at all.

"I'll walk you to the gate." Mary-Kate followed me, still not looking at me. It was still quite frosty outside. I should think about getting her a Christmas gift soon.

"Have you really thought about it?" I turned to look down at her. She was fidgeting with the gate—she was embarrassed and a little nervous to ask.

"About being a Catholic?"

"Well, being one for me so you can marry me?" She still wouldn't look up. It seemed I had caught her off guard. Tilting her chin up, I smiled down at her. In the cold breeze, a red patch had formed over her nose. Not even freezing temperatures could take from her delicate features.

"Of course. The last, what, five or six months have been amazing. You're incredible. I care about you a lot. Who else would I think about marrying?"

Had this moment occurred outside my house with my mother peeping out behind the lace curtains, she would have danced in delight at the lovely catholic girl getting a good grip on my collar, pulling me down and giving me a kiss.

"Goodnight, Joseph." She turned and ran inside without giving me a second to process what had happened. I watched her tiny frame disappear inside, red hair flying loose, and did my best not to dance the fifteen miles home so I would become known as the madman instead of the English one.

"I heard you said good things about me—which means you like me. So, be honest with me, Murphy." I pleaded with him.

"Alright, alright. You're spot on. There's no neighbour giving any of them a lift anywhere. She comes in here in the winter blue from the walk, and sits behind the bar with hot whiskey until she's ready. You meet her after your work so she's always in good shape by then. Please don't tell her I told."

"Thank you, Murphy. Why don't you pull two pints this time?" I slid the cash across the counter. "And no, I won't tell the five-feet small and scary barmaid that her boss admitted she wasn't invincible."

"Don't push it, lad, or you'll wear your pint"

I wish I had one of those cameras to take a picture of her face when she opened the door at eight in the morning on Christmas day.

"What are you doing here?" This was the first time I had seen her in pink – pale pink – and she was stunning. I must remember to use pink if I ever make her something in the shop.

"Merry Christmas, darling." She gave me a quick kiss and looked me up and down again. I had left home while it was snowing ninety minutes ago, and it had not stopped. She brushed snow off my shoulders.

"Joseph, what are you doing here?" She peeked back into the house. "We have the Christmas service to go to, and you know how Dad feels about you being here,"

"I am just delivering your present." That caught her

attention.

"Today? Not during the week?"

"Yup. Right now." She bit her lip and looked down at my empty arms. "Well, I hid it so I could surprise you."

"Well, I have your present to give to you next weekend, but seeing as you've walked all this way just for me, I would feel better if we swapped." Mary-Kate hated being handed something without handing something back; I had seen her unease last week when I passed on my mother's parcel and she had nothing prepared. I had expected her to insist on a trade, to try and divide attention instead of just absorb it. It took her a few minutes to locate it, but when she did come out, she also had a mug of tea for me. The lace curtain twitched and I could see more than one silhouette behind it. I gulped half of the tea and she held the mug while I opened her parcel. A song book with a matching scarf and cap.

"For walking to work." She was looking right up at me to see if I liked them. Saying nothing, I put them on and held up the songbook.

"So, what are your top picks for my walk to work." She giggled mostly in relief. She could put me on edge and call it entertaining, but did not appreciate it back.

"I already marked my favourite page," and there was that devilish smirk. Just as I thought: *Galway Girl.*

"Now that's mocking me with a gift—that's not very nice, Mary-Kate. Will you put this inside with the mug and cover your eyes?" Curiosity got the better of her, and she just stuck them behind the door and covered her face as quickly as possible. Mr. Ryan was behind the curtain too, because I heard him whisper, "*Jesus.*" when I lifted her gift over the wall.

"One minute." I flattened the frosty grass down with my boot to balance it, kicking the stand down, using my jacket sleeve to flick the frost clinging to it from where I buried it in outside the wall off.

"Alright, then." I felt sick with nerves as she turned around and lowered her hands.

"Oh Joseph! A high Nelly?" She took the whole bike in with her mouth wide open. "They're so expensive."

"But they last," I added. "The tires are good for the potholes, there's a basket if you go to town for messages, and look…" I turned the handlebars so she could see the daisies wound into the front of the basket.

"This is too much–"

"No, it is not. I decide how I spend my money and I choose that to be on making sure you are not walking eight miles to the village and back in the shit Irish weather, and not taking two hours to walk to town." Mary-Kate had pecked me on the lips before, but that morning I got a proper kiss.

"That cost a pretty penny." Her family were in the doorway taking from my moment with Mary-Kate. I shrugged, not sure what to say.

"Well, it's still freezing out and it's not slowing down. Stay in here 'til we head for the church, Thompson, and maybe the morning sun will have broken out by then." I nodded to show Mr. Ryan my appreciation. Seeing her happy with me seemed to soften him up the slightest bit.

When we left for the village, I got a taste of what married life would be that day—walking through the roads with Mary-Kate on my arm, chatting with her family and being the happiest man on earth.

6.

It was the beginning of spring when the railroad officially finished. Enough time for my father's business to return to what it was before the Civil War and be a reliable full-time job again. With her new bike, Mary-Kate began to visit my parents more and more, especially when she knew my mother was home alone in the morning before her pub shift. She earned my father's adoration for it. I had come home to see the photo albums opened on the table, to the tears of laughter being wiped as I came through the door, and the eerie silence and look of guilt on Mary-Kates face the day they talked about my brothers. I bumped into her nipping home on my lunch from the shop one day.

"Got caught up helping my mam out, so I'm late." She balanced her bike on the front wall and pulled back the blanket over the basket. "Wipe that hopeful look on your face, I've baked nothing. No time. For being late, I stopped and picked your mam flowers."

"She already likes you, there's no need to keep sucking up–" Mary-Kate pulled a bright red bunch of poppies out of her basket while I mocked her. Her smile faded quickly when she saw my face.

"Oh no, what? Is there a spider on them?" She held the bunch at arm's length, beginning to panic. My father had brought my mother back poppies only once since I had returned from the war. She preferred fuchsia and sweet Williams, so I had not seen them since then—not mulled over every horrific thing they reminded me of since then. Since meeting Mary-Kate, I felt I had woken up. Working two jobs preoccupied me, Friday nights at Murphy's distracted me. Looking down at the poppies I felt the dread and ice-cold shock, seeing something from the front grasped in her little hands brought all sorts of images to the front of my mind for the first time in months.

"Joseph—Joseph." I jumped and looked from the flowers back to Mary-Kate. "Are you alright, pet?" I felt uncontrollably angry, even reminding myself she didn't know, and she had picked them out of kindness did no good. I felt, though, that I should be entitled to be angry over them, and even if I was harsh, she would know it was because of what the war did to me.

"They are not coming into this house. Any other flower— not poppies." I snarled down at her, storming up the path and through the door, not holding it for her like I usually did. I would regret how unexplainably harsh I was to her later that evening.

"Okay, they're gone." She ran to catch up to me staring up at my face. "Can I ask why?"

"No."

"Well, that's not very sensible, it's one thing to get grumpy over them but not telling me why is just silly."

"Just forget it."

"Forget what?" My mother was making bread.

"I'm late because I was helping my mam out, so I picked you poppies as an apology, and Joseph has lost his temper over flowers and told me 'No poppies under this roof'. Now he won't tell me why." She dropped into the chair opposite my mother and playfully rolled her eyes at her.

"That's very silly, Joe, a red poppy. Go back outside and get me my flowers, young Ryan–"

"Don't." I stood looking out the kitchen window not wanting them to see me so angry. I couldn't stop it but part of me felt that, as my mother and my girlfriend, they should know to let it go because I never got angry.

"But Joseph, why—"

"Because they were everywhere in France." Both women jumped and flinched. "Those red poppies grew everywhere around the trenches and across the battlefield. They flourished in the blood and bodies of the men who were being killed, gassed and blown up." A few hours later, the guilt I felt seeing the tears in Mary-Kates eyes as I stormed out the kitchen and slammed my room door behind me was much worse than the guilt, I felt for not holding the door.

"You're twenty-six, Joe."

"I know, Father."

"You stormed into your room and slammed the door like a six-year-old."

"I know, Father"

"Slammed it on your mother and your twenty-year-old girl— who was crying from guilt, by the way."

"I saw that, Father."

"You made her cry because she didn't know about something she never could have known. Was that right?"

"I know. I have a lot of grovelling to do."

"Well do it quick. She cares a lot for you and the longer this goes on, the bigger the apology you owe her."

I walked slowly to Murphy's that night. I wanted to make sure it would be closing time when I got there. I only had to wait for ten minutes outside when the last punter left, and Murphy came to bolt the door.

"Joe. Good to see ya. You need to come in. I thought someone had died when I saw her face." That did not give me the confidence he thought it should.

"That's my fault."

"Ah. I see. Well, from what she tells me, your parents are all for it and hers aren't. Count your stars her dad did not see her in tears because not only would he demand ye broke it off, but your head would also be on a stick by the front door as a warning to all her other suitors to come. I don't know what you did, lad, but I'll head out back and leave ye to lock up. You broke right through her barrier and somehow snapped that heart of steel, Joe." That was Murphy's polite and nice way of letting me know he wasn't impressed with me either.

Inside, she was cleaning down the tables and standing chairs and stools up as she went. I went up beside her, and began to do the lifting part for her. She froze up for a minute, glanced out the corner of her eye and continued without a word. It was like that from one side of the pub to the other until she began to get her stuff to leave.

"I understand that you're mad, and I completely deserve it."

"I'm not mad." She stayed looking down, finding stuff to unnecessarily adjust to keep her hand busy. "I'm waiting to see if you still are."

"Well, I'm not." She nodded, and the room lapsed into silence again. "I'm lots of things. I'm guilty, I'm sad, I'm upset at myself and I'm confused as to what happened to me today. Most importantly, I'm hoping and praying you will talk to me or even just listen until I fix this." She peeked up at me looking me right in the eye for a minute—the longest minute of my life—making her mind up. Finally, she nodded and led my back to the corner booth we always sat in.

"Mary-Kate, I care for you a lot. I should not have shouted at you or gotten angry over something I can't even explain. I'm foolish and I am sorry. So incredibly sorry. I got so mad I couldn't make sense of anything and I made you cry and feel it was your fault and I swear on my two brothers I will never do that again." She started crying, again. I sat there dumbfounded. I had never seen tears run down her face before, and I never thought I would be the cause of even one.

"Sorry." She wiped her face with her cardigan sleeve. "I felt stupid for not knowing why. Then I felt stupid for crying in front of your mother like a little girl. I've felt stupid all evening for not following you a few minutes later and fixing it. I won't bring up anything to do with the war again, not for stories about your brothers or to see your medals or to brag about you to my cousins. Not anything."

"I don't want that, Mary-Kate," I whispered. She looked surprised. It was a change from upset, I suppose. "I can't talk about it for some reason, I feel sick and like I'm charging into battle with my heart beating and my palms all sweaty slipping on my gun not knowing if I'll survive. It reminds me of all the soldiers I walked past lying in the field dead. Or the faces of the boys on the other side that I shot in close range. It reminds me of the feeling of being shot or the pains of frostbite. But worst of all, it reminds me of what happened to my little brothers. I can't think about it. I was walking around in a daze of nightmares before you, Mary-Kate. You woke me up, and when I saw you holding something that reminded me of… it all, the horror set in, and I couldn't stop it." I looked down at my hands clenched on my lap trying to regain control. After a few seconds of trying to breathe though the flashbacks, a small hand cut through my vision, wiped my face and pulled on the elbow of my jumper to get me to give her my hand.

"Okay. Well, now that that's out there it was no one's fault, really. You can't help your reaction to it, no one blames you. I can't even imagine the things you've spoken about. And I didn't know about the poppies. So, we're both in the clear. It was a misunderstanding, that's all. And we've cleared the air now—like a proper couple." We smiled at each other through teary eyes.

"Seeing you cry breaks me." She gave me a small laugh and took one big breath to clear it all. "But hey, a grown man just cried his eyes out in front of you, that counts for something of an apology?" I got a good tight grip on both her hands leaning across the table to kiss her. Sitting back, she peeked around the pub.

"Murphy isn't here giving you that creepy wink?" I shook my head. "Oh, my. How untraditional and improper of us."

"A woman of your class and vigour—no one would believe it."

"Good." This time, the silence was content and happy.

"And you know, I meant it. You can still ask about my brothers, they had whole lives before the war and I'm trying not to let how they died ruin those memories."

"Good." Her chin went back into the air with her confidence. "Their names can go back on my list." She went to stand up, but I pulled her down.

"What list?"

"My family will come looking for me if I'm not home soon, locking up doesn't take that long–"

"What list, Mary-Kate?"

"And if Dad sees us alone in here, you'll be dead and then I'll be dead, and we can't be a couple if we're both dead. The Galway girl and his daisy will be no more."

"Mary. Kate." She blushed. She was embarrassed.

"List of names."

"What names?"

"Names of family members that are important and sound nice." I processed that for a minute.

"Like a potential-baby-name list?" Her entire face turned tomato red, and I laughed the hardest I had all year.

"Oh, shut up Joseph. You announced your plans of conversion and marriage after a few months, and I haven't said anything about babies I just let that slip so don't even–"

"Alright! Alright, I've stopped." She put out the candles and we stepped outside. I escorted her to the side door where her bike leaned against the wall.

"Goodnight, Joseph."

"So how many babies have you thought about–"

"I'm leaving now! Good luck and good riddance." I jogged to catch up with her and give her a quick kiss. She didn't shove me away, but she did let out a little *Hmph.*

"Goodnight, Mary-Kate" I called after her. I could have skipped the whole way home that night.

Taking one last look at it for courage, I snapped the box shut and stood tall. There was no reason for me to fear a Catholic church, or a priest or parishioners. Mr. Ryan, on the other hand, was a terrifying ordeal to face. I pictured many scenarios in my head, all ending with him flying over the pews to throttle me in the doorway. Shoving it in my pocket, I straightened my tie and walked into the kitchen.

"Going somewhere nice, Joe?" My father nodded to my good shirt and trousers.

"The catholic church's Easter Sunday mass." I shovelled down my porridge to have something to do instead of thinking of all the reasons to just forget it.

"Did Mary-Kate ask you to?" My mother's eyes were literally round in her head like the comic strip of the paper.

"No, and please, I don't need to hear reasons not to I'm trying to convince myself to go. Her father scares me."

"Her father should. It's a father's duty to a daughter to scare the shit out of men." My father stared into space thinking of the father he would have been to the little girl he never had.

"Well, you're in the right place." My mother nodded.

"What?"

"I saw the way Rick Ryan looked at you that day in town. When he kills you for taking his daughter, his family's approval and now a seat at his church, they have all they need to bury you right there."

"That is not funny, Mother." My father wheezed into his cup of tea, and I decided to leave before there were any more mentions of Mr. Ryan looking like he wanted to kill me.

My timing was off, and I was glad I left early. They were getting ready to start when I went in. I stood down the back to be respectful. I knew half the church-goers from the pub, or the site, and they looked at me, grinned, and pointed to Mary-Kate's father. The ceremony started and I looked ahead at the priest. There was no way he didn't see me at the back wall, and I appreciated his willingness to let me stay there. Bit by bit, the whisper I was there crossed the aisle, and after a few sneaky looks back to me from the front rows, the Ryans glanced back to see what was back there. Four faces of surprise and one of murder. I saluted and turned my attention back to the priest. Stepping on her brother's feet, Mary-Kate made a point to her father and the parish by crossing the pew to the aisle, rather than slipping out where she sat by the wall and marching down to stand with me at the back.

Whether it was cutting remarks to drunks or a silent statement, Mary-Kate knew how to get her point across. After five minutes, standing still got to her and she decided on coming in front of me so she could throw her whole weight back onto me. I wrapped my arms around her waist and she brought her hand up to hold onto them. A point was being made to Mr. Ryan; I think. We stood like that for an hour, but people clearly didn't get used to it, as they kept turning to peek. Mrs. Ryan nearly started dancing in her seat when she saw us. After the ceremony ended, we waited outside for her family.

"What were you doing–"

"Please just trust me and I will tell you on Tuesday at lunch." Her family were approaching.

"But that's so far away," she whispered.

"I know the answer." Mr. Ryan glared up at me.

"Pardon?"

"To the question if you were brave or stupid. You're stupid." I just nodded in agreement with him.

"Mrs. Ryan, lads, do you mind if I accompany you to ye're after-service drinks in Murphy's?" They all agreed to me coming, and Mr. Ryan went a darker shade of red at not being asked.

I walked ahead of him to the pub, sat between his two sons at the bar, and drank up my Dutch courage before tapping him on the shoulder and asking him outside. It was difficult to do with Mary-Kate staring at us, but the pub filled up and I seized my chance.

"What now, Thompson? It better be good, because you've annoyed me all day and I'm close to putting my foot down with Mary-Kate–"

"Mr. Ryan, sir. May I have your blessing to ask for your daughter's hand in marriage?"

7.

"What?" I looked at my feet, cleared my throat and cleared my speech in my mind.

"Sir. I love your daughter. And she loves me. You've said yourself, she is past the traditional marriage age due to her temper—the temper that made me fall in love with her. I have a good and stable job, and when I can, I work two jobs. A plot local to my parents has come up for sale, and I put the last of my railway wages on half of the payment for it. I will build us a house there. I have the means and ambition to give her a good life. I will convert, marry her a catholic and raise our children catholic. She will never have to want for anything. Out of respect to you, I have not hinted to her I am going to ask—I did not want to get her hopes up in case you said no. But please; I adore her, I will give her everything she could ever want, and I will do anything for you to approve."

He stared at me in silence for a few moments. I could picture Mary-Kate in my mind telling him he would catch flies and tried not to smile. It was a very uncomfortable silence, and it killed me to stare him down, but he had to know that I was serious about us.

"Well, that was quite the speech, Thompson. I do not like you. I do not like the thought of my girl with an English man, a protestant. But you've got nerve – I can't deny that. Whether or not I like it, I think Mary-Kate would refuse anyone else to spite me if I said no., I expected to refuse my blessing when she came home with a ring on her finger. You've got me by surprise." I reached into my pocket and pulled out the ring to show him.

"That's one hell of a rock, lad." He didn't call me Thompson. "A plot of land and a ring like that for my girl?"

"Yes, sir."

"It's a relief to see you're just as invested. You've my blessing, Thompson. But if one of my grandchildren look into the gate of a protestant church, I'll kill ya." I nodded and pocketed the ring. To my surprise, he offered to shake my hand.

"When will you do it?"

"We have a lunch planned for Tuesday. I'll ask her then. Please don't tell anyone—"

"By anyone you mean my wife. Of course. I want Mary-Kate to have all the surprise and happiness on Tuesday. My wife couldn't keep a secret if Jesus himself descended from the sky and personally asked her."

I looked around the plot, making sure I had everything for the picnic. I told Anthony to wait at Murphy's and tell Mary-Kate to cycle out past my parent's house for half a mile. Any minute she should be here. I had bunches of daisies scattered around the blanket. A small path and the blanket for eating with all her favourites were laid in the centre of the circle. Mother wanted me to make a heart out of them, but that was too obvious for the proposal.

She arrived in a pink dress, hair falling out of its bun and face flushed. After she kissed me, I tugged the pin out and let her hair fall to her shoulders—I loved the little bits that fluttered around her face in the summer breeze. Time flew sitting with her. I listened to her latest gossip, laughed at her Sunday night punter stories, and tried not to be too obvious I was staring at her the most nervous I had ever been in my life.

"Joseph, the sun is starting to set, it must be after six." She peered at her watch. The face of it was always on the inside of her wrist for some reason.

"Mary-Kate–" She stood up, waving me off.

"Don't convince me to stay, I'll be late for my shift."

"Mary-Kate–"

"No, no. I've never been late to Murphy's and I always hold that over him. I've to go."

"I cleared the evening off with him."

"I need to pin my hair back as well when I get there – you what?" I stood up beside her.

"I love you, Mary-Kate." She stared at me, shocked and then jumped up to kiss me with the biggest smile I had ever seen on her.

"I love you too, Joseph." I smiled down at her and grabbed her left hand.

"That's good to hear." I bent on one knee and watched as her face changed when she realised what I was doing. Pulling out the box, I pushed the lid open with one hand and held it up. "Will you marry me?"

"YES!" She high-pitch screamed so loud my mother told me that night she heard her at home. One ring on a finger, lots of tears later, and we sat back down with her head on my shoulder and our hands clasped together while I told her of all my plans.

"This is our plot of land for our house. Me and a few of the lads will start digging the foundations tomorrow. I got your father's blessing. Only he and the priest know. The priest knows, because after I got his blessing, I booked my christening next Saturday morning straight away."

"You've it all planned perfectly."

"I hope I make it to my christening; my mother may kill me for not telling her anything." She giggled.

"So will mine."

"So now that you know my plans, can I hear the name list?"

"I guess so. For girls: Eliza, Eileen, Áine or Saoirse. For boys: Simon, William, John and Anthony. Whatever ones we agree on, if you like them."

We married in the middle of August 1922. Not too cold for an outdoor reception, but not too hot because Irish people hate too much heat more than too much frost. We had our ceremony in her local catholic church, where I had been christened a few months before, where generations of Ryans had received all of their ceremonies and blessings. My parents happily sat on my side of the church with rows of empty pews behind them. Mary-Kate's family took the front row, the extended family took five rows all to themselves, and then the locals to Murphy's filled the remaining seats.

The week before, Mary-Kate had been waiting for me when I came home from the shop with my father. She ate dinner with us and then we were left alone for her to discuss her main reason for calling. Both her and my parents wanted me to consider wearing my medals on my suit. Any soldier would be in ceremonial uniform with all their success pinned to their jackets. But they understood if I said no. After considering their points on why I should wear them, and thinking how good it made me feel that one night in Murphy's I caught Mary-Kate bragging about me, and my time on the front to her cousins up from Cork, I agreed. On one simple condition.

While I stood in the church waiting for her to arrive, nodding to people who saluted me and trying not to panic over everyone openly staring at my medals, my father sat proud as punch in the front pew with Simon and Will's medals pinned to his suit. I thought many times about what they would think of Mary-Kate, the jokes they would make. Will and Mary-Kate teaming up against me; they had similar senses of humour. Simon just openly mocking anyone who crossed his path. My throat was beginning to feel tight at the thought of them both stood beside me as my best men in a perfect world, but thankfully my bride made her entrance before I could get too upset.

I was not the type of groom to shed a tear at the sight of his bride or lose his words. Looking at her walking down the aisle, arm in arm with her father, in the palest shade of pink I had ever seen with daisies in her hands and in her hair, I felt the proudest I ever had in my life.

Back in the village, Murphy turned the street outside into an outdoor reception, complete with wooden doors for a dance floor. As I twirled her around and around for our first dance to *It's a Long Way to Tipperary*, I heard whispers from onlookers of how romantic our entire relationship was. The Catholic/Protestant thing gave it a 'forbidden love' feeling. It wasn't often that comments on our relationship were so poetic and kind, so I decided I would remind myself of those two words the next time I was criticised for not leaving her alone to find herself a simple life.

In true Mary-Kate fashion, she tipped off the trad band and our first dance changed pace into Galway Girl. Everyone laughed, drinks were put down, and there was dancing through the whole village that entire night. Nationalities were forgotten, religions were forgotten, and political scores were forgotten and that one night everyone was just happy to celebrate our marriage.

And yes, even Mr. Ryan danced.

"It's so pretty here, Joseph."

"I know." Kerry was everything Ireland was painted to be on the postcards the local sold. Grass very green, water very blue and accents very thick.

"We must promise to come back here again."

"Of course, dear."

Mrs. Ryan suggested our week honeymoon should be in Kerry after staying there one night travelling to visit family. I was so glad she had. It was unlike anything I had ever seen, it seemed to be otherworldly.

"Sorry for the wait, Sir and Mrs." The hotel receptionist was a very jolly woman dressed in emerald green. I bet the American tourists loved it. "What's the name on ye're booking?" Mary-Kate stuck her chin in the air, took my arm and answered before I could.

"Mr. and Mrs. Thompson."

8.

I did not know it at the time, but the first five years of our marriage would be the smoothest and most uneventful of our lives. Not that we had issues among ourselves, but politics, society and world leaders would change everything for us. By the time we rang in the New Year of 1927 with our family in Murphy's, we only had two of the six names left on Mary-Kate's list.

John came the first summer after we married, and was followed ten months later by his first sister, Eliza. Both sides of the family were carried on to the next generation, on Mary-Kate's insistence we keep things fair. Her father looked like her had a full lemon in his mouth when he heard his first granddaughter's name could not be translated into Irish. That all melted away when he first held her. Mary-Kate took motherhood in her stride, and somehow became even more incredible than I could have imagined.

Just as Eliza began to crawl and move about on her own, Mary-Kate was pregnant again with our twin boys who she insisted were a sign from God, and insisted on calling them Simon and William. The day they were Christened, my mother cried all throughout the service and the lunch. I told my wife the day they were born that the tears in my eyes were from happiness at her decision on their names… that was the first actual lie I told my wife. They were a good six months old before it didn't hurt me to call them by their names. I had begun to see their personalities—little William was bold and daring like my Simon and little Simon was a quiet and reserved baby like Will. That made the guilt of feeling as though I was trying to replace them fade. By their first birthday, calling them by those names made me feel as though I had honoured them.

Of course, by their first birthday, Mary-Kate was waddling around, eight months pregnant with both her and my own mother running after her begging her to let them take over the small celebration at Murphy's. Eileen came the week after the birthday party, three weeks before expected. Already having four children, Mary-Kate had quietly given birth, not waking a single child in the house and was sitting up, both her and new baby wrapped in fresh blankets—handmade by their father of course, like all their first outfits – by the time the doctor arrived.

Eileen's Irish twin, Saoirse, arrived the day of Mary-Kate's brother's wedding, the week before Christmas. She was in tears at the thought of taking from his day, but Anthony and his new bride could not be happier for us and for the chance to be the first to hold the baby. Mr. Ryan beamed with pride telling all the wedding guests his granddaughter's name, and in time it became very clear he favoured Saoirse the most, purely for her name.

In Spring 1927, we sat together on the back doorstep after getting the doctor's call to confirm her seventh pregnancy. Friends and neighbours always complained to us how the older our children would get, the easier life would get, as they could do things for themselves, but we felt it was opposite, adoring having a newborn to hold and tiny clothes to wash and mend. Days flew by with tantrums, bottles, nappies and work. It was the evenings, after eight, when all were in bed that we got time to ourselves.

"Mam was right," Mary-Kate whispered. "That I'm with my seventh. Mothers always know, right?" She leaned closer and I wrapped my arm around her waist. There was still a light winter nip in the air. "She reckons we have our full set now." Typically, Irish families were made up of five to seven children and, although she was admitting we had hit the magic number, Mary-Kate sounded ever so slightly sad.

"Does she now?"

"Mmh." We stared out at our vegetable patch for a few minutes longer in the quiet. It was her pride and joy. She fed the family through three of the four seasons of the year with her schedules and rotating.

"So, are you happy with 'our full set'?" She sighed, calculating her answer. If she had to think about it, she was thinking of a way to tell me something without really saying it out straight.

"Well, we manage our six much better than some do with just two." She wasn't wrong. We were by no means rolling in money. We did have to budget, and it took me a long time to convince her that baked goods were perfectly fabulous gifts, even more than something she could buy me. She gave up the pub after our twins; she did not miss it, though, as she revelled in her children, her house and her vegetables. Mary-Kate took all the hard work of serving a full pub of drunks and the fire she had to have to deal with them, and poured it into making our house the smoothest-running one in Munster. I wished I could spoil her with clothes and things, but she seemed delighted in our children's drawings, reading their story books and managing them all in town with a baby attached to her with a daisy printed shawl. Our house was built and well-sturdy from war and railroad wages. With my father retired from old age, I worked the shop alone.

The wage supplied the food and fuel we needed. It supplied

the six (soon-to-be seven) children we had, and left a little a week aside for our children's birthday and Christmas gifts. We had it comfortable. I made their clothes in the shop when I had time as it was cheaper, and Mary-Kate's brothers ran a construction company together and were happy to fix anything that broke. Not to mention Mary-Kate was a dab hand at fixing and mending herself.

"We certainly are, darling." I paused and she said nothing. "But…"

"But I love having our children," she whispered, turning her face into my shoulder to hide her embarrassment at admitting her secret. As if she thought I would not give her anything she wanted in this world. "I love our children so much and I love seeing their little personalities starting to show and how they start to look like either of us the older they get. I love our full house and the stories I have to tell you when you come home. I hated sending John and Eliza to school, and even though I have another four at home and the fifth coming it feels so quiet during the day and– "she broke off and sighed. She sounded on the verge of tears and stopped to gather herself.

"Darling, we will be done having children and growing our family when we are ready. Not when we've been told we have enough. We will be done the day you hold one of our newborns and tell me 'I'm done now'. Not when you feel you have to be done. You don't have to be embarrassed to tell me you like having a family with me. So, another one, or feck it, another seven; I will never tire of our family or of watching you be a mother." I felt her softly smile into my shoulder.

And grow our family we did. Áine was with us by the winter of 1927, and we announced our eighth pregnancy at Christmas dinner. Our fourth son, Anthony, did not get to meet either of my parents. The summer of 1928, my mother passed away in her sleep and, out of heartbreak, my father followed her two weeks later. They were, of course, buried in the closest protestant church—my children's first experience of a protestant church. Where my parents happily joined us for our children's catholic ceremonies, Mary-Kate's parents did not set foot on protestant ground for either funeral.

In those two weeks, I lost most of my respect for Mr. Ryan. I expected him not to come; I expected him to stop his wife. I did not expect him to kick up and argue with his sons on their attendance and support of their sister who they knew adored my parents as much as I did. I was furious he tried to convince Mary-Kate to wait with him, alongside our children, at Murphy's for me to be done with the service and burial.

"This is too far." I tried to reason with him at our kitchen table, Mary-Kate sitting beside me, staring at her father, horrified he was fighting his cause at such a time.

"How? You knew of my little tolerance for our... differences." He had the audacity to look me up and down. "I accepted the solution of you converting, well on paper, anyway. I hardly see you at any services, but my daughter and my grandchildren will not go into a protestant church. I told you as much when you asked for my blessing, boy."

"They are my family, and I will bury my father tomorrow. He was not ill; he did not look sick or tired. He passed suddenly and I would like to say goodbye to him with my family. With his family."

"Absolutely not." He stood to dramatically walk out of our house. Mary-Kate breezed past me, shoving baby Saoirse into my hands. Our other children were under the watchful eye of kind and unbiased neighbours, all of whom brought dishes upon dishes of food to last us an entire week.

"Listen here." She grabbed him by his elbow and spun him to face her. "Mr. and Mrs. Thompson showed me nothing but kindness, something you never gave Joseph. They showed you, Mam, John and Anthony kindness. Asked nothing of me. Never complained about their son's catholic wife or children. They were front row at every ceremony and service. They never passed comment or even took sides in politics and stayed out of fights and arguments. They were good people, Dad. Do you know why? They saw other people around them—not nationalities, not religions, not sides—people. Mr. Thompson told me the day of our wedding that at last he had gotten the daughter he always wanted—and he treated me as such. Our house is full of the furniture they passed onto us or made for us. So, I will be front row with all of our children and with my husband at that funeral, and if you are not there you should be ashamed of yourself, because that means you're only half the man Mr Thompson was for not attending his funeral, and not even a fraction of the man to be buried tomorrow." He stood with his face gradually reddening with anger as we went inside to be with our family and to grieve with my parent's friends.

"Thompson?" He had stopped and turned in the front door. I said nothing and raised an eyebrow. "You know I said I would not tolerate my grandchildren setting foot on protestant land. How. Dare. You." He spoke of my children like there was something wrong with them for being at their grandmother's funeral and for going to their grandfather's tomorrow. I marched down the small hallway, grabbed him by his arm and dragged him out the front gate.

"I will not tolerate my family being spoken of like that. As long as you have that attitude towards my children for saying goodbye to their grandparents, you are not welcome in the home I built from scratch for my wife and my children."

He was nowhere to be seen, not even in the pub, the next day. Mary-Kate swore she had lost all respect for him. And when we next met at the christening of Áine's christening that September, she refused to let our children take the sweets he offered them.

"This family is not selective, you love and be there for all, not some. You can still see them, just not in our house like Joseph told you. Your bad attitude has been tolerated for too long; good luck to you now that people know you've crossed one of the soundest men in the country—and his wife." The entire pub was silent while she spoke her few, but severe, words to her father. Her mother made a point of calling twice a week to our home after that, and even suggested what to do with my parents' empty house.

"Other ladies and I from the parish could make it our little project for the next few weeks. Both of you are of quick to lend a hand to others and help out despite your eight babies, so many have offered to chip in. You go through the place and take what you want, put out what needs to be burned and we'll clean it, give a lick of paint to whatever needs sprucing up and you could make new bedsheets and curtains. You'd rent it out in no time."

And so, the project began. I shoved a box of medals and photographs into the bottom of our little wardrobe, and put some scarves, hats and gloves into the kids' rooms. Extra layers for the winter never went to waste. I left out my mother's cardigans and father's suits for the parish women to take as a thank you for their help. Every one of them adored Mary-Kate and our eight children. Many of them pulled me aside to tell me how much they admired what I changed for her and how I worked so hard to make them happy.

By that Christmas, we had a new and young family renting out the house. I left the rent money to Mary-Kate for whatever she or the kids needed. She took great pride in being the landlady, and the extra money allowed her to expand our family even more. We left it two years to settle into our new lives, though. Eight children, two houses to keep standing, and I now had an entire shop to run alone. I wanted to wait until one of my own sons were old enough to train in the books, but the pressure was on, and I was away for longer periods of time. Telling myself it would be years to go yet before John, Simon or Billy were able to join me, I hired a local boy.

"The summer of 1928 when I buried my parents marked the end of a rather peaceful and easy time for myself and my family. In 1929, we felt the slight pressure of the Wall St. Crash in our little piece of Ireland, but we survived the nineteen-twenties rather well. They were to be the best years of my life, as from then on, times only got harder.

9.

Rivalries between myself and the community spiked in March 1930. My eldest daughter, six-year-old Eliza, was rushed in the door by John in hysterics.

"Daaaaad!" I cannot describe the chill down my spine of hearing genuine fear in one of my children's voices—that was a sound I had hoped I had left in France, and hearing it from my son rattled me.

"Oh my God, JOSEPH!" My wife's shriek made me feel sick. I picked up Anthony and Áine in either arm and ran in the back door. I had worked hard to finish work early that Friday, and I was glad I was home to be there for my children when they came home from school.

When I got to the little hall by the front door, Mary-Kate was frantically trying to pry open Eliza's little hand, dripping with blood.

"John, what happened?" He was an ashy-grey colour, staring up at his mother with wide eyes. They had seen blood before, scratching up their knees running around playing, but never had they seen it running bright red down someone's arm before.

"When I left class to walk home, she was sitting outside the school wall screaming crying, so I just grabbed her arm and ran back with her."

"Go to the kitchen and make you and your mother strong and sweet tea. You both need it. Take the biscuits out the pantry and divvy them up with your siblings. Keep them in the back yard. You did good, boy, looking after her." He nodded and set his jaw off to finish his job being a good brother for even longer, and rushed to look after his mother too.

"Joseph, she won't let me look." Mary-Kate looked like she was going to be sick. I picked Eliza up and carried her into our room. Mary-Kate ran to the dresser, routing in the bottom for a spare towel or old item of clothing.

"Eliza," I cooed, trying to get her to relax a bit. "Eliza, I can't fix it if you don't let me. Open your hand, petal." After hugging for a bit, trying to catch her breath she loosened her fingers. I was glad she let me see it. It would have been for her own good, but it would have broken my heart to force her hand open. The gash in her soft little hand was deep, and blood was running from it still.

"I'm taking her to the doctor." I pressed the towel Mary-Kate passed me to her palm and scooped her up, marching out the door.

"Joseph, so help me, God, you get her to tell you who did that." My wife's shock and fear turned to blinding rage as I carried Eliza out the front door.

"Now, six stitches in there, Eliza. My goodness, young Miss Thompson, you are brave." Dr. Mulligan praised her as she hiccupped on his surgery table. "I've treated grown men who have had worse reactions to one. Six stitches!" He wrapped it in gauze and gently tied it shut.

Standing he gave me a wary look. It wasn't often he treated small children for such severe injuries. Knowing myself and Mary-Kate so long and looking after our eight children, he was just as concerned as I was.

"Spare gauze and some mild pain killers, Joe. Split them in half for her and keep it iced." I nodded. "Did she say anything on the way here?"

"No. I hate to say it, but she seemed embarrassed, hanging her head when Mary-Kate and John were with her. Can I talk to her here away from the fussing at home?"

He nodded. "Take all the time you need."

After he left, I knelt down in front of her and tilted her face up.

"Petal, I don't know what's happened, but you got hurt. And as your dad, I really don't like to see you hurt at all. Not even crying. I know there was a lot of fuss at home, so while we're here will you tell me what happened?" She looked apprehensive. "You know I won't get angry, petal."

"I forgot my prayers." Her voice was scratchy from crying. "My communion is in May and we had to know off our prayers, but I mixed them up and got them wrong. Mr. Prendergast was so angry he shouted at me in front of everyone for being a stupid little prod, right at me up the top of the class and he got angrier when I cried." She started crying again. "I didn't mean to cry for getting in trouble, but everyone was staring right at me, and I felt so stupid, and I couldn't stop crying so he got angrier, and he hit the switch off my hand so hard I felt it in my heart, Daddy, I felt the pain shooting right in here." She pointed with her good hand right to her heart.

"There's nothing to be upset or feeling stupid about, lots of people forget things. To tell ya a secret..." I leaned in and pretended to peek over my shoulders. "I hardly know any of them." I pressed my finger to my lips and shushed really loudly, getting a little giggle. I picked her up and shoved her spare gauze and pain killers into my pocket. "Don't you worry, there will be

85

no more misunderstandings with Mr. Prendergast. I'll drop you home and go sort things out with him right now." Eliza waved to Dr. Mulligan on the way out. He was clearly waiting to see what happened, but I left ten pounds on the table inside the door and told him to keep the change. I was trembling with anger so much I was afraid if I stopped walking, I would put Eliza down and punch the nearest wall.

At home, John was still very serious about his jobs, standing right beside his mother, coaxing her to have another biscuit.

"Thank you pet, but mammy's full, you can have it."

"John, take your sister to the kitchen for her tea." He jumped to the job, holding her good hand and leading her down the hall.

"Well?" Mary-Kate leant forward in the armchair, still a place grey colour. Our daughter's blood had stained her blouse sleeve.

"Mr. Prendergast shouted at her at the top of her class for forgetting her prayers. He even called her a prod—a professional man with schoolboy insults. She cried because everyone was starting at her and he felt it was right to crack her hand open."

"Bastard." That was the first time my wife had spoken with so much venom in her voice.

"I'll be back in a while; I'm going to have a... discussion with him." She nodded to me and headed for the kitchen while I went out the door again.

Twenty minutes later, I stood on his front step, across from the school. His wife answered the door looking shocked as she took in my blood-stained jumper.

"May I speak with your husband, please?" I smiled at her. He might mess with people's families, but I was a bigger man than that.

"Ah, Mr. Thompson, good." He stepped outside and shut the

door. "I was hoping we could talk about your delinquent daughter. I don't know if it's the protestant showing in her, but she needs to behave and learn her pray–"

I grabbed him by his navy tie and dragged him three times around his front yard. I made sure to keep my grip at the knot so when I lowered my hand, he ran around his yard three times like a man imitating a horse.

"OI! LET GO OF ME, YOU ENGLISH BASTARD!" I finally pulled him up right, glad to see his fat face blood-red from pressure.

"I'm giving you the courtesy of just feeling how mortified and embarrassed my daughter was today, but if you ever lay a hand on any of my children like that again I will inflict the same injuries on you, do I make myself clear?" He nodded, trying to swallow. I let go and pushed him back into the ground and walked away before I could change my mind and punch him until I felt I had done my daughter justice.

At home, Mary-Kate put my supper on the table and said nothing. All children, except John and Eliza, were in bed.

"Well done today, John. You did me real proud. What a little man you are." I ruffled his hair and he smiled. "Now, off to bed lad, you've to go to town with your mother in the morning." He gave us both a kiss on the cheek, and even kissed his hand and gently patted Eliza's gauze where she slept on her mother's lap. He stopped to look up at me before heading off to bed.

"Why did he call her a prod? What does that mean?"

"It's just a silly argument between different versions of religion. It has nothing to do with you, and don't worry about it. Only unintelligent people like that teacher use language like that. Ignore it, son, and always be the bigger man, like you were today looking after the house for me." I winked at him and ruffled his hair.

I cleaned up while Mary-Kate held Eliza, rocking ever so slightly. We brought her to our room for the night, guessing she would feel happier in with us after the day's events. Mary-Kate was still an ashy colour. Blowing out the candle, I leaned across Eliza and kissed her on the forehead.

"I swear to you, none of our children will hurt like that again while I breathe."

"I know," she whispered back. After a few moments she asked, "Will things ever change, or will people always use our children's surname and family history against them?"

"We can't control the world, love, but we can raise our children to be bigger and better people than the ones they're going to encounter." She locked our fingers together over Eliza's rising and falling back, and had a stressful night's sleep worrying over something she had never before considered for our children.

That Sunday after mass, the atmosphere in the pub was different, just like the times before I met Mary-Kate. A divide between them and us. It seemed despite having no injuries the Prendergast's were getting away with their exaggerated versions of Friday night's events. Sure, who would people believe—an Irish educator or an English tailor. Teachers were held in as high regard as priests, and it seemed I had crossed an invisible line. I technically hadn't laid a hand on him, just his necktie. From then on, our children no longer walked around the pub smiling and waving at our 'friends' and neighbours. We stayed to ourselves, in our booth, just as content but just as wary.

10.

"But why not?" Saoirse whined up at me.

"I can't go because I've some things to fix up." I patted Saoirse and Eileen on the heads, making sure not to ruin their neat and tidy braids. Today was their end-of-school-year Céilí dance. After spending extra time after school every Friday, they were ending the year with a little show for all the parents. I, however, could not go.

"But you always ask us to show you what we learned after our lessons." Eileen had joined in, trying to guilt me into going. It was not easy to explain to two four-year-old's that although I wanted very much to be there, I was not welcome at their school anymore.

"You remember when Eliza hurt her hand and had two weeks off of school until Mammy and me felt it was okay for her to go back?" They nodded in unison. It was easy to see how people mistook them for actual twins. "Well, I spoke to her teacher the day she hurt it to find out what happened, and we couldn't agree on what happened to her. Teachers are seen as very important, and you don't… disagree with them—but I did. Mammies and Daddies are not supposed to disagree with a teacher. But I did over Eliza's hand." I tried to explain it to them without telling them why I had been pushed out by everyone locally. Even the shop's trade had slowed.

"And you disagreed with the teacher?" Saoirse narrowed her eyes. She was always that little bit too sharp and caught on to things Mary-Kate and I tried to slip past her.

"Yes."

"So, go talk again and fix it! That's what Mammy makes all of us do and it works." I smiled down at her.

"I wish it was that easy, dear." They pouted and looked sadly at each other. I could not believe my luck in having a family so close and caring for each other. It killed me to let them down time and time again the past few weeks because I was very aware; I was not welcome in the school hall. "But I've seen ye practicing and I know it will be so good; I have two presents waiting for when ye come home." The disappointment vanished and was replaced with the excitement of presents.

"Let's go, girls." Mary-Kate had Áine and Anthony ready to join her at the little show. She pecked me on the cheek and gave me a sad smile before heading off with the girls, waving over their shoulders at me. She felt guilty that our so-called friends had a sudden cold demeanour towards me now. I did not care for the social standard of respect for teachers or thinking they knew best, beating children for being forgetful or wrong instead of helping them. When things were taken too far and one of my children got hurt, of course I was going to fight their corner. The last few weeks I was ignored walking to town and back, waiting for my children outside of the church and in the pub at Sunday lunch. The few people who still came into the shop were curt and cold, not wanting to seem too friendly and clearly sour I was the closest tailor they had. They seemed to think some punishment for my bad behaviour of putting Mr. Prendergast back in his place would snap me back to normal, but my family came first, and I was not backing down.

Mary-Kate had tears in her eyes last Sunday when it was announced in the pub by the school headmaster that any Irish parents with time next Friday, could come and see a little Céilí by their children to show off their year's progress, with a sly glace towards me. I waited at the gate until they'd gone around the bend. I headed back inside and found John in the door staring at me.

"It's because you dragged Mr. Prendergast around his front yard like a pony in clear view of his neighbours?" I nodded waiting to see his reaction. "I know you did it to stop Eliza being hurt again—I saw her crying and I would have gone too if I knew where you were going. Just because he's a grown up and a teacher doesn't mean he should get to hurt people's sisters like that."

"Exactly, son." What a little man he was going to be. "Now, let's go repair the dresser in time to have the lady's tea ready when they're back." I worked quietly with him in the back yard, watching Simon and Billy play. As much as I expected the reaction I got, it made me nervous how long it was sticking. I walked my children to school every morning now and waited until they went through the gate. I was not foolish enough to think someone would not retaliate and take it out on them. I was a very big war veteran; sides would not be evened up with me.

"Hello?" Unfortunately, a familiar voice was echoing down my hallway. I looked through the back door where there was the slightest view of the front. Mrs. Shea from the village was peering in the door. I went quickly to get to her before she invited herself in and started looking around. We had nothing to hide, but she was a gossip—a creative one at that—and Mary-Kate had enough to deal with without her spreading lies.

"Hello, Mrs. Shea." She went to step in, but I was down the hall and had her stopped before she made it, and it was too difficult to get her to leave. This was the worst thing about the summer; the doors had to be open so the air inside wasn't thick and sickly—and anyone could just march into your kitchen taking it as an open invitation.

"Hello, Joe." She smiled at me. I braced myself waiting for it. She never called without an agenda. "I was wondering if we could have a chat?" She glanced back up the hall making it obvious she wanted to come in. I remembered the times I had listened from the living room window to Mary-Kate play stupid like she didn't get her hints, so she didn't have to be invited in. I simply nodded and stared back at her.

"Of course. About?" Her face turned sour for a minute, but she regained her fake niceness and started off.

"Well, I'm worried about Mary-Kate and the children, you see. I know you care for them so much and, really, I admire a man who's so open about loving his family—its few and far between you find that! So, I thought I'd speak to you myself, because you're such a lovely, quiet man, Joe, and I know you'd appreciate my concerns for ye. It's just this little stalemate or rivalry really can't be good for her at all. She's looked so sad and solemn since it's happened, and I bet the children pick up on it—she's their mother, of course they do—so from what I've heard—now I'm saying no names—but from what I've heard, a simple apology some Sunday in the pub to Sean Prendergast, and all would be solved. You're an army man, Joe Thompson! That little girl came home in hysterics I heard, and she needed the doctor and all and you went into protective mode and now we're here! Now a pint and a chat between yourself and Sean, and all would be back to normal, I'm sure!" She smiled up at me. That greedy kind of smile from someone who wants something, in her case, to be a part of the story.

I mulled over what she said and tried not to laugh. Mary-Kate carried on as normal except ignoring the rest of the pub on our Sunday dinners with her family. She even told me the relief of not having to fake her interest in the other ladies' gossip and blatant rumours. She hated how they picked a new target each week and was relieved they paid her no more attention. Except for the few occasions in the last two weeks that I could not attend end-of-year school functions, my children had been unaware of any change at all—except for John.

"I don't think that will happen. He quite seriously hurt a six-year-old's hand over prayers. It was completely uncalled for. No other child had that severe of a punishment—none of the embarrassment or the stitches. He's finally left my little girl alone after the year of yelling and torment. I'm quite happy with how things have turned out." She huffed and folded her arms.

"Now, Joe, when ye first got together ye were the talk of the county. All the things you did for her, the expensive bike, the religious change, and now it seems it's wearing off. You don't even come into the church unless it's something big! I don't know now if married life has opened your eyes and you've had a change of heart, now–"

"Let me stop you there!" I cut her off before she could fully spin her story for the next gossip session. "I love my wife very much. I'd do it all again. But regardless of which religion it is, I don't think being front pew and shoving your head up the priest's arse is going to make any difference on your Judgement Day. I'd prefer to put my time into my family and being a good husband and father, then spend one hour a week pretending that I'm perfect when I'm not. I can't say what the big importance is on priests and teachers in Ireland is, but I won't be part of it. Doing wrong is doing wrong." I kept my voice as cheerful as possible, pushing back the fury at this lying, little woman who would tell the parish I said a whole bunch of things I did not.

"Well, you chose to live here!" She put all her niceties aside.

"Blend in, Joe! Forget all your protestant upbringing and go to mass, forget Sean was one of those lads that gave you a hiding years ago, for the sake of your children's education, and forget this silent rivalry with the community because we all value good teachers that will beat the education into the ones that won't put effort into it and APOLOGISE!" I stared at her for a minute processing her loss of temper.

"Sean Prendergast was one of those lads, was he?" She realised her slip up and gulped. "See I had no idea who they were until now. Looking at your face I wonder how you knew... unless it's something to do with your husband and Prendergast being thick as thieves?" She looked away, trying to find an excuse to leave. "So, is that what this is? He lost his temper with a child called Thompson and decided to teach her a lesson? I won't have my children on the receiving end of arguments and fights that have nothing to do with. We don't do politics in this house. You can tell the whole pub that on Sunday!"

"You can leave now." John had come around the side of the house and opened the gate for her. She looked between us, aghast, and then marched off with her nose in the air, reeling with all the things she had to tell. John slammed the gate behind her.

"Thank you, son." John smiled up at me, proud of himself.

"I don't like her." Simon was peeking around the side of the house with Billy nodding beside him profusely.

"That makes four of us." We headed inside for our tea, and I made sure to shut the front door behind me.

That evening, after I gave the girls their new summer dresses and all children were in bed, Mary-Kate and I made the decision to pull the girls from school. Few girls around were sent to school anyway and it seemed Eliza was used for political example, but not John. The boys would have a better chance of not being flaked to the bone than they would. Mary-Kate would teach them to read, write and look after themselves at home. I could do maths with them in the evenings. We would look after our own and make do like we always had.

My apprentice retired from the shop out of the blue, no explanation so I enlisted John for the summer. Spending all the extra time with him amazed me. He had so many traits that reminded me much of men he had never met or heard about. We found our new routine in a few weeks—all three girls delighted over no longer going to school, and now spending time with their mother. She was quick to remind them it would not be an eternal summer holiday.

Coming back into August, we were sorting out the next years' worth of school supplies. Áine would join them this year, so we needed seven of everything—not to mention Anthony starting next year and the little baby bump Mary-Kate had again. While we sorted the books one night, she pulled out the old biscuit tin with the renter's money in it. We had plenty to do that school year and I was relieved that losing half my business gradually had not hit us so hard. I noticed a wad of pounds rolled up and tied in the corner of the box.

"What are you saving for?" I was confused. We recycled all the baby clothes and I fixed them up if needed. Her bike was in fine condition; nothing was broken or shabby looking.

"Never you mind." She wouldn't look up at me. I nodded and said nothing, but it bothered me. Was she unwell and uncomfortable telling me? I always made it clear that I wanted to help her if she needed anything. I started to keep watch of her. She seemed fine, but I knew she was keeping something from me. A week later, I noticed six of our seven children seemed giddy or excited—like they knew something. John looked just as confused as I was.

It was in the third week I found out. The evening of our eighth wedding anniversary, I came home to a covered object on the table where my dinner should be, and my favourite cake. I gave her the new earrings I thought she would love and gave her a funny look.

"This year I had a really good present idea." She looked so excited, she even forgot to open her earrings. "Open it, open it!"

Mary-Kate had seen an ad in the paper to order a sewing machine. I had the old one at the shop, and it worked, but these ones were easier to use. She had been paying it off weekly at the post office and the children were all excited when it came in, and they had to help her hide in their room.

"I thought you could keep it here for home bits until the other one is fully done and then take it to the shop?" Now she looked nervous. I hadn't given much of a reaction. There were eight faces peering around the door at us. Smiling to myself I pick up my pregnant wife and spun her three times.

"AH JOSEPH! PUT ME DOWN! PUT ME DOWN!" She was screaming and laughing. The kids started to giggle looking at their parents acting like kids. I swooped her down like I had seen in the movie posters and kissed her.

"Thank you darling—I love it!" I lifted it to the counter, and we all sat down for the cake. Screw everyone else—my family was worth a million of what having a few mates at the pub was.

That winter, we welcomed baby Hazel. Mary-Kate had no more names on her list, so I suggested calling her Hazel because the strange colour of Mary-Kate's eyes was one of the first things I noticed about her. After eight christenings with my parents and our friends attending, the ninth one seemed so empty. Only my in-laws were invited, and Mary-Kate didn't even ask her father to the house after. We celebrated ourselves with a special dinner my mother-in-law helped to make.

I had come to appreciate Mrs. Ryan a lot since my mother died. She was so apologetic when her husband would not let her come to the funerals, and she always gave me a long hug and a kiss on the cheek when we met now. She seemed hurt by my entire family being gone as much as I was. I suppose she did not have to live it and could not see how I would come to peace with them all being back together while I had the burden of grieving their losses. Nonetheless, I had come to adore her like my own mother, and I loved her even more for not caring about Mary-Kate's societal status.

"You make her so happy, Joe," she whispered in my ear, hugging me at the door that night. "And I am so grateful to you for that." She kissed my cheek and stepped back, holding my face in her hands. "My third son." She smiled the kindest smile I had ever seen in my life and headed home, Anthony waiting at the gate for her.

11.

The only event of 1931 was welcoming our last son, Thomas, into the world. He was a premature baby and gave everyone a large fright the day that Mary-Kate, seven months pregnant, woke up bleeding. Having her so far away in hospital for a week of observation killed me. I had not been away from her for so long since we started dating, and I felt guilty leaving my old mother-in-law to watch nine children under the age of ten. I felt the line should be drawn there on our baby count; Mary-Kate felt otherwise.

"You said until I'm done. I love having our babies, and I am not done!" She sulked in our bed, where she spent another week on bed rest. My rule, not the doctor's.

"You could have died, Mary-Kate! What if the baby died? That would kill us! If it's not safe–"

"It was one out of ten babies, Joseph! Besides, you promised." Her eyes were particularly green when she glared at me, reminding me of the night we met ten years ago. As much as I wanted to argue with her over having another baby next year, I knew how stubborn she was. I was going to lose anyway, and with nine children running and crawling around the place every morning, waiting for me to tell them what to do, I had to pick and choose my battles.

I was completely right about losing the no-more-babies fight. That next year, baby eleven arrived with an unusual name. I kept Mary-Kate under a watchful eye that pregnancy, and she had the free time to read the paper and listen to the radio more now that our three eldest daughters could cook (under her watchful eye) and our three eldest sons helped around the house. Billy even stepped up to do the clothes washing in the river, not being afraid to do 'one of Mammy's job's'.

During her bed rest, she followed a lot of interesting stories—one in particular of a couple running across America. Admiring their conviction and their help giving back to the people suffering during the Great Depression, she found one more name she really liked.

"Bonnie."

Mrs. Ryan stared at her in shock. "You want to name my new granddaughter after Bonnie and Clyde?" I heard Simon chuckle from the next room.

"Not after her—I just like the name. I had never heard it before. How unique too, a girl called Bonnie in Tipperary!" Mary-Kate was delighted with her new idea. Mrs. Ryan slowly looked over her shoulder at me and I just shrugged.

"Baby Bonnie?" Was all I could say.

"Baaaaaaby Bonnie," Mary-Kate cooed from behind a ridiculously newspaper." As fierce and as tough as she liked to act, Mary-Kate made one hell of a cute pregnant lady.

When Baby Bonnie finally arrived, there was quite the que of little men and women waiting to meet the baby that kept Mammy in bed for weeks and kept them on their toes with all their extra help around the house. John insisted as the oldest boy, and head of the house when I was absent that, he should get first hold. With Saoirse and Eliza lecturing him about the baby's head, all the children gathered around him at the foot of the bed, delighting over her.

"Joseph?"

"Yes, my darling?" she giggled quietly.

"I think I'm done now." She peered up at me through her lashes.

"Really? All the asking I did last year and now just one baby later you're done?" She stared at me for a minute, pretending to reconsider and then firmly nodded.

"You infuriate me, Mary-Kate Thompson. And I adore you for it." She beamed as I leaned in to kiss her forehead.

Bonnie was a very spoiled baby. She barely started crying when someone scooped her up, cooing and wiping the tears falling from her big blue eyes. John, Simon and Billy all took unnaturally mature and grown-up stances on looking after her—even going so far as to help with nappies and late-night bottles. Eliza showed interest in learning to make her baby grows and hats so she could doll her up any way she saw fit. And that is exactly what gave Mary-Kate and I the time to sit by the radio and listen with worry to the latest news of a change in political power in Germany.

"This won't end well, Joseph. I have a bad feeling."

"I know, darling. I feel that too."

"Is this how things were…"

"Before the Great War? There were some tensions, but it really hit me out of nowhere. I was a young fella, I wasn't paying attention to the news. Maybe if I'd read the papers and listened to the radio, I'd have been ready, but it feels like one day it was just something happening, and I had to go."

"You fought in the war?" Saoirse was standing in the hall door with her mouth wide open. "I never knew!"

"Never knew what?" Billy stuck his head out the living room.

"Dad fought in the war!"

"Like the Great War?"

"Yeah!"

One by one, my children filed into the kitchen—the Irish twins holding the youngest. I glanced to Mary-Kate who looked nervous and panicked—like she didn't know how to avoid what was brewing.

"No way, Dad!"

"What was it like?"

"Were you there in all of it?"

"Did you stay in the one place or move?"

"Did you ever shoot someone?"

"Enough!" Mary-Kate stood up. "Wars are not cool stories to tell or gossip about. And I expect you to be old enough to know better than to ask a person if they ever shot someone, Áine Thompson!" While she gave out to our children, I pushed through them to our room. I hated to think about it, but these were my children. They knew nothing about me that they didn't see themselves, some of them didn't even know anything about my parents. I knew for sure that none of them knew I had two brothers. I got my mother's old box of medals that I took from the house out of our wardrobe and brought them back to the kitchen.

"I mean, in all honesty. How insensitive!" Our three eldest boys were just the same height as Mary-Kate now even though they were only coming up on ten. She was more than capable of handling all eleven.

"Sorry, Dad." Simon, our quietest, was the first to speak up.

"Actually, I think ye all should know a little about it." I left the box on the table and smiled a little at Mary-Kate. She seemed caught off guard, but moved to sit beside me and hold tightly onto my hand. "Sit, please. You all know about war and, I guess you can at least know I was in it—but no stories." My medals made their way around the table, Billy holding them like they were going to break into a million little pieces. There were eight very sad and glum faces when I finished giving minimum details. They had to know about the world, the bad parts too. So, if another war brewed from all the changes and trouble going on in Europe, they would not think it was hugely heroic to run to the front of it like two people who were very important to me had done before.

"What are those medals for?" Eileen peered into the box, eyeing what was left.

"They were my brothers' medals."

"Brothers?"

"You had siblings?" The most painful part of my life came up. I pulled out the one blurry photo of my parents, my brothers and I, taken in 1913.

"This photo is over twenty years old now, be careful with it. This here is Simon, he was a year younger than me and the little lad is William, two years younger. I was of age when the war started. Simon joined in 1915 and Will joined in 1916. Here are the letter and telegraph announcing their deaths. Both died on the battlefield. And – they were, um…" I found it hard to describe them. To say what they were like, tell stories and describe their personalities.

"Is that why you never told us about any of this? Because you lost them?" I patted the back of Eliza's hand and nodded.

"I didn't find out they had died until I came home, my parents didn't want me to lose hope on the front."

"Did Mammy know them?" Anthony finally contributed after soaking up the evening's stories.

"No, pet. I met your dad in 1921. His parents were still so sad-looking, and he seemed so lost. Bit by bit he livened up, and his mother and father got great enjoyment out of me making fun of him, our dates and planning a wedding. Losing your family like that is not something you get over so quickly, you know." Our children all looked around at each other, imagining what it would be like to not see each other for years and to find out that the other had died a while before and never have known.

"This box is going away again. I'm proud to have it but I can't look at it every day, especially that photo. No more questions, or listening, Saoirse, ok?" Eight heads nodded in unison.

"Good, everyone off to bed now, so."

That night of stories and medals played in my mind in September 1939. Times got better with the Great Depression wearing off, but fashion got faster and faster, and now I opened my shop two days a week for the little custom I got. With the rent from my parents' house and John, Eliza, Simon, Billy, Eileen and Saoirse all working in shops or on farms, contributing to the food shop and helping at home, we stayed afloat. We managed. But I hated it—not working, being so still, feeling like I was under Mary-

Kate and the children's feet. Since the Great War, I had supported my family, and now I felt I was merely contributing. The guilt I felt over making my brothers proud, and competitive boys who ran to the war came back as guilt for not providing for my family.

That is why when the radio announcement came in, my wife knew how I felt, and she looked up at me with huge teary eyes.

"Joseph, no," she whispered.

"It's a steady wage and a steady pension. It will make things easy for us again. For the children." I couldn't look at her, she would be able to convince me not to enlist.

"But you were born and raised here–"

"But I am English, darling. They will let me enlist. Not contributing to this family is breaking me. We can't depend on our children who are starting out because I can't do anything else. I have to go."

Two weeks later, I stood by my front gate, bag packed and my family staring at me.

"Honestly, Joseph, this is ridiculous. There is no need for it, it's so silly. You do contribute so much to this house and our children. After all those years of two jobs and then owning the shop yourself, enjoy the time to relax and stay, please." Mary-Kate did not give up once. I walked forward to hug my children, one by one telling the little ones to be good and the big ones to help out so much it was like I wasn't gone. I was touched to see even my sons had tears in their eyes. Lastly, I hugged my wife.

"The wage, darling–"

"Screw the feckin wage," she whispered back. "What am I supposed to do if anything happens…" She couldn't finish speaking.

I gave her the longest, most meaningful kiss I could and then walked away without looking back. I would never go if I looked back at my hysterical wife in the arms of my eldest son... if I saw my daughters with tears streaming down their faces or my sons hiding theirs with their heads bowed, trying to be strong for the rest of the family.

Neighbours and friends who had said little to me in past years stood by their doorways and outside the pub to nod goodbye to me as I passed them. Dislike me as much as they did, they understood why I went, and I was grateful they respected it. My family were in good hands in Tipperary and that was all I needed, like the last time I left. Twenty-five years after I first left for war, I headed off down the same roads to the same unknown destination, knowing I could never see it again, and it hurt me twelve times more...

12.

5 October 1939

Joseph,

Darling, I cannot tell you how relieved I was when I got your letter. I've scrubbed every surface in the house waiting to hear from you. The children actually had happy tears when it arrived in the post—the boys practically threw tantrums because I did not wait until they had come home so we could all read it together. Lesson learned.

I am delighted to hear you are not in any trenches this time. When you return home again, you won't have to deal with those leg pains again. Most people seem to believe it will be over by Christmas. I've taken to going to mass every night so I can pray for it.

My father has started calling to the house. He wants me to send his regards. I think war has made him realise how petty and stupid his actions were and he now regrets them. We could have a Christmas with both of you at the table this year.

It's funny—every time the children do something funny, I think to myself I should write it in my letter to you but now I'm sitting here all I can think about is you—having you home. I don't want to seem like a silly little barmaid anymore, but I put some summer skirts into the bottom of your wardrobe last week and the smell of your cologne out of the wardrobe made me so happy; I sat down and cried. John found me and I felt so silly, but he was so kind. I don't know if it's the month of worry since you left, but he seems like such a man now. I think having so many children I *hardly have the time to properly look at all of them and notice how they change.*

John stays up at the radio with me at night. He's also started at a construction company—they let him have Friday mornings to walk me to town. He tells me half the town knows you left for the wage, for the employment and now feel the guilt of taking a husband and a father from his family... Good. I hope it eats them up at night.

Saoirse has become heavily involved in politics; she collects papers and listens to the radio all day long gathering information. She's building up a heavy letter of all the politics happening in war although it will all be month-old news by the time, she sends it. Not to mention you're in the war and know it all before we do, but I'm letting her cope how she wants to.

I suppose asking you to stay safe is rather silly, but try to, darling. Fingers crossed I can kiss you at Christmas.

All my love,
Mary-Kate.

Oh, my darling—wars don't end in time for Christmas.

25 December 1939
Dad,
I hope you're ok. I know you well enough to know that you wouldn't tell us if you got injured out there, so I sincerely hope you're well. To be honest, that might just be the news to finish Mam off. She used to potter around the house distracting herself and she was always cheery going to town as well, shooting her evil glances at people she knew were unkind to you. She's so down now. She's all hunched over and quiet now. It might not be very manly to admit it but it's scaring me. That can't be good for her

at all, and I don't want her unwell. Is there anything you can think of that I can do to cheer her up or remind her to try to be positive? The younger ones are picking up on it, and I'm afraid this sadness will spread like the flu from the little ones right up.

The job I have is doing grand. It's nice to be able to help out at home. Mam would never admit it, but with your wage and mine things are so much easier. She wants you to think being out there is pointless and come home. I'm working with a few lads whose fathers did the railway with you. They all send their regards and want you to know they always had great respect for you. They also say Mam need not want for anything, if something needs a mend, they'll help. There's a bunch of ladies Mam used to know calling for tea bringing food and baked stuff. She was a bit short with them at first, but now she's happy to let them in. Billy is pure delighted with the constant flow of cakes and breads. So is Anthony, but he likes the colours in them. One of the women calls around and shows him how to bake. There's help and apologies being offered on all fronts and we have nothing to complain about at all. I hope that brings you some comfort out there.

Eileen and Saoirse are fair good with the machine now. Eliza is taking a bookkeeping class so the three of them can open the shop up and have another wage in. Eileen is gone all women's-rights and got annoyed over the 'Thompson & Son's' sign—'cause you have daughters too. Simon repainted the sign to 'Thompson & Family' and she cried. Everyone seems to cry really easily these days. I suppose she was looking for something to think about and he fixed it too quick, so she had no more distractions.

Can't wait for you to come home.
Love,
John.

He needs to take her to Murphy's pub for Sunday dinner and get her mother to visit every day. He needs to keep her busy.

7 March 1940

Dad,

We hope you're okay. Winter is gone and it's spring now. It's funny that the house is not full of flowers that you buy for Mammy all spring. The winter without you was so horrible. It was always dark; we had to be inside a lot, and it really made us notice you were gone.

No one sits in your chair at the table. Not even visitors. Mammy won't allow it. She turns on the radio to see if you're coming home. Grandad had gotten sick and can't shake it at all— so Mammy is twice as worried.

Eileen, Saoirse and I have opened the shop. It's mainly repair work but it's another wage for the summer. We all want to save up and buy Mammy a nice present, really try and cheer her up. John is down in Cork for the building company; he's very busy. Billy and Simon are sharing looking out for mammy. Simon is being trained up in diggers. Billy's cheeky reputation has stopped a lot of people from taking him on to train in something.

Bonnie wants you to know she hasn't gotten one spelling wrong since before Christmas. Anthony made Mammy a chocolate cake and wants to post you one soon (Billy is going to take it and eat it but in your next letter please say it was yummy). Thomas and Hazel are learning to ride bikes from Uncle Anthony. Áine is starting a book collection.

That's all our news for now. Stay safe.

Love,

Eliza, Saoirse, Eileen, Áine, Hazel and Bonnie.

"Bloody hell, Thompson." My comrade was peeking over my shoulder. "That's six names on that list there—how do you feed all of them and a wife?"

"Those are just my daughters." I carefully folded the letter. "I have five sons, too." There was a low whistle and laughter in disbelief.

"You look after all of them? Where do you find the house for them? You must by a countryside fella. If you were in the city, you'd never afford renting two apartments."

"Yeah, something like that." I lay down and turned my back to sleep. Young lads like that took solace in talking about their families, like I used to with my brothers. But when it's your children you've left behind, it somehow makes this Hell even worse.

23 September 1940

Joseph,

Hello, love. I'm writing to tell you my father has died. He was very unwell all year and very weak. It hurt to see it dragged out for so long, but he's at peace now. Mam has moved in with me. I feel like a young girl again, sleeping in a bed with my mam after a nightmare. She brings me great comfort. We are both missing our husbands very much.

The children are trying so hard to keep me happy. I feel like an awful mother. They've all matured so much, you'll hardly recognise them when you return! Hazel started a wall to show you all her correct spelling tests when you get back. Some of them are wrong, but I don't have the heart to tell her she didn't get them all right. Simon sits down with the four little ones every Friday, and they hang their pride and joy up for you to see.

John is doing so well for himself; he's even courting now. I'm not trying to be funny, but he has found himself an actual Galway Girl. You have something in common with her! Sadie from up the road is getting in a television set soon, she said we can watch the news instead of listening to it. She said they show footage of the war; I think I'll feel better when I see it because I imagine such horrendous things.

Old Murphy asked me to do Friday nights for him again. I don't know if it's from pity of looking at me like a lost puppy or genuine need, either way I was glad for it. It's nice to just chat about absolute nonsense sometimes. It also helps Mam, I think, doing the bedtime run with the kids once a week and having gossip to hear when I come home.

Stay safe and do come back to me soon. I hate this hollow feeling.

Love always,
Mary-Kate.

My wife wanted to guilt me into returning for her. It's not so simple, my darling.

3 January 1941
Dad,
HAPPY NEW YEAR! We all wished for your safe return as soon as possible! The boys bought Mam a television set—the smallest one. We thought it helped her to cope, but she's being lying. Seeing those machines they use—I get a cold shot down my spine thinking of it. I can't believe you have to go up against that. How horrendous.

I somehow doubt you want to discuss the war machines in letters from home, though. Sorry. Saoirse keeps giving out to me for rushing in headfirst, running my mouth and then upsetting people. She said the other day I would turn out like Billy; I was so offended!

I've been thinking after the war I want to be a politician! Why can't a woman run for party? Look at how brave Countess Marckevitch was in the rising, she is so inspiring. I've also been reading books on brave women—I have decided I shall not conform to society's norms! Mam giggles when I use those words, but she says she supports me. Apparently, she's laughing 'cause my chin sticks out when I get all passionate like yours does. I am grateful for my handsome Dad's trait, of course!

I've been experimenting in the shop—not to any cost, of course. But in magazines and on the television, I saw women wearing trousers! How wonderful! In war time they have been called to step up and are allowed to do things like that. I'm making myself a pair and I can't wait to see what Mam thinks. Maybe she'll want a pair too? If she does, that's half the battle on getting Eliza to allow me to sell some women's fashions.

I'll let ya know how the new fashion trend takes at home.

Love ya,

Eileen.

Yes Eileen, your mother will want a pair. Anything to keep you happy and buzzing around. You could stitch a circus tent, for all she cares.

19 August 1941

Dad.

Hello. How are you? I'm good thank you.

Teacher says letters have to be started like that. I think its silly 'cause you haven't sent me a letter asking how I am, so why am I answering you?

I go back to school in two weeks. I can't wait to see my friends again and swap sweets and lunch. Simon always gives me sweetie money for Fridays. Sometimes Anthony makes cupcakes, and I can take some too. I don't mind as long as I get chocolate.

Now that I'm ten, I'm going into a new room again. I'll be in the senior room from now on—the oldest in the school. Eliza says I'm a little man now—I guess I should start going shopping with Mammy like all the other boys did.

The picture on the back is Bonnie's—it's of all of us after the war, she says. I want to see the planes on the telly, but Mammy says no, I've to be older. But they sound really big, are they?

Bye again,
Tommy.

For an eight-year-old, Bonnie was very good at drawing. Maybe we had a baker and an artist in the family.

14 February 1942
Joseph,
Hello, darling, I hope you're well. I realised the other day you had not yet said you were injured, and realised with the weapons they're using you must be and have kept it from me. I'll deal with that secrecy you've developed when you get home!

Simon, Billy and Eliza have moved out, and are renting an apartment in town together. Eileen and Saoirse and on the floor below them. They're all so grown up. Five of them left all in the one go. I still have five, but the place does feel rather empty. They want to send money home like John does; I can't stop him up in Dublin from posting it, but I want a better grip over them, so I can yell at them face to face. They're all too good at heart.

Eileen has started quite the trend in the family—every girl has a pair of trousers now. Bonnie refuses to wear hers. She loves skirts. She's always trying on my ones. We have a right little lady in that one. I'm afraid if I blink too fast, she'll be in front of me with rouge and lipstick.

In John's last letter to me, he was talking about proposing to Sandra. He was happy she got on so well with everyone at Christmas, he has a deposit on a ring, and he was planning on asking her today!

Happy Valentine's Day, by the way. Another year without you. I'll never take a day with you for granted again, my love. You are quite literally my missing piece right now.

Come back to me soon, my Galway Girl,

Love always,

Mary-Kate.

Happy Valentines, my dear. I wonder will John marry soon; I wonder if I could get the time to go to it. I haven't asked for any leave yet. But missing this would hurt more than visiting for a few days and leaving again.

5*May 1942*

Dad,

I hope you're warm and safe. Everything is plain-sailing here. We have the shop doing very well. Eliza is training me in the bookkeeping; she got offered a position managing in the post office. She's very fancy altogether now. Since moving out, I feel I have become Eileen's second mother. She dives in headfirst and I'm left to pick up the pieces. I also got the shop a contracted client. I impressed a new stud farm that's opened in the county with sample riding clothes, and they've signed a five-year-

114

contract with us!

I was so glad to hear Sandra offered to leave the wedding until the war was over. I was looking forward to you coming home but getting you for a few days and giving you back might have killed Mammy. So, I love you, but I don't want to see you until you're home for good.

I know this is rather short and sweet, but you get twelve letters every time and I don't want to distract you too long and you get shot or something.

Love you so much,
Saoirse.

My sweet Saoirse. She made me chuckle thinking I was sat on the battlefield reading her letter. I was glad she thought life here was so simple.

16 May 1942
Joseph,
I don't know what to do... I can't hardly think of what to... how do I...
Dad,
Simon here. Eileen was taken by the Magdalene sisters in town. Someone told them Eileen was three months pregnant. She hadn't told us yet. No one can go in to get her even though she had three older brothers—they said it has to be the man of the house and slammed the door in our faces even though we explained the situation. They won't let us see her. They came to the house and dragged her out by her hair, Bonnie said. Mam is in pieces and I think Granny is going to have a heart attack. Dad, what do I do now?
Please tell me how to fix this,
Simon.

No. I joined the catholic church for my family, but no way were they deciding on what happened to my children—or grandchildren – pregnant from wedlock, or not.

"Thompson, are you alright?" A few of the lads shouted to me while I marched across camp. I rapped on the bunker door until it was opened.

"One-minute man." I pushed passed him and marched up to the table.

"Sir, I need to urgently request leave." My seniors looked me up and down. "Urgent leave? Name and number." I rattled off my details quick as I could. "Wait outside please, Thompson." I got curious looks from boys sat outside.

"You're trembling, mate, are you alright?"

"Fine. Urgent family issue, that's all."

"Look at his hands, he's trembling."

"He's always quiet, I wonder what's happened to piss him off."

"Thompson. Inside, please." I hoped they decided to give it to me, because either way I was leaving. "One week enough?" "With all respect sir, no. To get home in time a week is not enough…"

"Are you opposed to sitting in a cargo plane, Thompson? You'll be there in no time if you're not shot down."

13.

Seamus Murphy was much too old to be cleaning the tables and shining the glasses in his pub anymore, but he had his pride about him. His father had opened this pub and worked in it until the day he died, he never left it, and neither would Seamus. He was happy to have help from his grandchildren now and then, and to have Mary-Cáit back in the pub at least one night a week. Being good at pulling pints wasn't the only think that kept a pub full, you had to have the personality, and Mary-Cáit Thompson had it in buckets. Well, at least she used to.

Thinking of her and her husband, thousands of miles away, and her children growing up faster than she seemed to believe, made him sad. It was only Tuesday; he wouldn't see her until Friday evening. He liked to keep an eye on her, know what was happening. He met her when she was just sixteen and started working for him, saw her dish out as many slaps as she got, fall in love, get married, and celebrate the births of eleven children in the walls of his pub. After Joe left for the war, she stopped coming, her children got awful dull and drawn looks to them and she hardly ever passed through the village on another one of her wild missions. Although he would never say it, because a man like him was a man of very few words, he worried for her like she was his daughter.

When he had the idea to get her in one night a week, he hadn't expected her to accept with so many young children, but also with so many grown up children all working too. The shock of getting word she would be happy to was nothing compared to the shock of the woman that turned up at the backdoor the first Friday.

In eleven pregnancies, Mary-Cáit held onto none of the weight, but where she used to look elegant and slender, she now looked frail and weak. Instead of glaring at anyone who had the nerve to meet her eye, she stared up at him with a blank and empty expression. Under her eyes were two very dark shadows, but her eyes themselves looked red, as if every night she went home and cried herself to sleep. She was hunched over, slightly frowning in worry and unconsciously chewing her bottom lip. There was hardly a trace of the woman that used to be there before Joe left. Mary-Cáit was not struggling with Joe being back in war. She was breaking. Crumbling away, leaving nothing of the fierce and feisty woman she was behind her. She looked about ten years older than she actually was. She might not light the pub up on a Friday evening with her wit and brazing charm anymore, but there were a lot of people who made it their business to call for one drink to chat, but really to check up on her.

Troubling himself over her, Seamus went from window to window checking all the locks, the back door and finally the front. It swung right open. The spring in door handle had gone, and he needed it fixing—he would have to call Simon Thompson in the next time he passed on his way to work and get him to fix it. In the meantime, he would have to manually pull the heavy iron deadlock back out to be able to let the punters in tomorrow.

By now, he was hard of hearing, and did not hear the steady steps walking up the middle of the village past his pub, but when the shadow passed over him, he glanced over his shoulder, not properly seeing the face of the figure, to greet him.

"Good evening." He shook the outside handle. He would need a knife from the kitchen to try and slide it out.

"Four in the morning, Murphy. I'll say good morning to you." Seamus thought he had lost his mind. All the thinking of Mary-Cáit and her family, he must have conjured the man up in his mind, made himself hear things in his old age. But, turning around, he saw what could not be mistaken—standing six-foot-six in a British army uniform, was Joe Thompson, walking through the village like he had been doing it regularly the last three years.

"I- wha- you- Joe!" Joe stopped and looked back at him. Where Mary-Cáit looked ill, Joe looked empty and numb. Thinking back to the papers, the radio and those horrible machines he had seen on the television set, Murphy knew why Joe decided to cope by switching off.

"Yes, Murphy?"

"You're home?"

"Only for three days. Took two days to get to Wales – get the ferry, the train and walk into town—three days I have and then I'm headed straight back."

"Oh, Joe." Murphy teared up with relief. "Thank the Lord God, saviour above that you came back for her."

"So, everyone knows then?" Joe's voice had an eerie dead sound to it.

"Well in all fairness, it's hard not to notice it! Half the parish comes in here on the weekends." Joe stood staring at Murphy, clearly confused.

"But she's only three months, Murphy. She wouldn't be showing yet, so how could half the parish see it?" Seamus' heart skipped a beat.

"Cáit is pregnant? But you've been gone—"

"No! Eileen is. She was taken by the Magdelines and they won't let her brothers discharge her. Wanted to know what I thought they should do, so I came straight home to go get my daughter!" Murphy relaxed after nearly giving himself a heart attack. "Why did you think I was home for Mary-Cáit? Half the parish can see what?"

"Well…" How was he supposed to tell a man who returned to war to feed and support his family, that his being at war was slowly destroying his wife? "She's not coping. She looks fierce unwell and not herself at all. She's a completely different woman, Joe! She moves about and does things for the sake of the children, but I shudder to think what state she would be in if she didn't have a reason to try every day. All the money in the world from you, or John, or Simon, or Billy, or any of the girlies in town makes no difference. She needs ya, Joe. Being apart is killing her." He watched the battered and bruised family man nod slowly, processing all this information.

"I knew she was struggling, but I didn't realise she was unwell too."

"Too?"

"Why do you think I never came home on leave before, Murphy?" Joe sounded like a broken man. "I don't want to miss my littlest ones growing up, I don't want to miss my eldest becoming their own people. I sure as hell don't want to be apart from my wife Murphy. My biggest fear is seeing her and not being able to walk away again—becoming a deserter. The look on her face when I first left haunts me every time I blink—I'm dreading doing it again." After a few moments of silence, Murphy managed to muster up his words again.

"Well, you're a strong lad Joe, not just 'cause you're an army man. You've always stood tall and persevered, no matter what the cost. You'll get through this war and be back to her for good again. Just make sure the next time you come back, it's for good."

The two men nodded at each other.

"I know you wouldn't, but keep seeing me quiet, would you Murphy? I don't want the local paper standing outside the Magdelines when I leave with Eileen."

"I won't, on the condition you get in here for a drink and a meal. I'm sure I can muster up some sort of sandwich. The nuns won't answer the door before seven anyways; you'll wait three hours and then people will see ya and there'll be spectators. In here and refuel now, lad. Besides, those old nuns put up a fight, you'll need your strength. Oh, speaking of, can you get this bloody door open…"

Murphy was not wrong. I was glad I had sat it out for a few hours in the pub; it was nice to just sit there, looking around and remembering for those two hours. I took the bike he said had been abandoned out the back and cycled my way into town, gathering a lot of double takes. The first glance was for the British soldier on the bike. The second was for 'Joe Thompson, home from the war?'

The Magdeline sisters' convent was in the centre of the town; a soulless stone building with massive concrete steps up the front of it. I could feel the eyes boring into the back of my head as I climbed up them. As much as I missed them, I prayed none of my four children renting in this town were up yet to see me here, unannounced. I did not want to be distracted while I was collecting my daughter.

At five to seven, the milkman came and switched the glass bottles, shamelessly looking me up and down several times. At seven on the dot, the door opened, and a middle-aged nun stepped out to grab them. I stood tall, cleared my throat and moved to stand in front of her. I would be totally respectful, and there would be no drama to be had with this.

"Sister, good morning. My name is Joe Thompson, I am here to collect my daughter Eileen Thompson. I believe she was taken into your care a few weeks ago. She is only early into her pregnancy yet." She stood staring at me, shocked.

"She is about this high, green eyes, black hair. One of your sisters… collected her from my wife Mary-Kate Thompson. Both are very strong-minded and outspoken, I'm sure one of ye will remember them. I have no doubt it was a quiet affair. All of my girls are very feisty. Now do I wait here, or would it be more respectable and mannerly to wait in the hallway?" She gathered herself and straightened up, getting a nasty look on her face. She was getting ready for a fight.

"Yes, Mr. Thompson. Your whore of a daughter was taken in by us because she had defied God and his way, and got pregnant from wedlock with a man who wasn't even in town to hear their little fling gave him a child. She is in here to repent and pray away her awful sin until the child is born, where it will then be adopted to America. Then she may go on about her life in sin and shame asking God every day for his forgiveness." My blood was pounding in my ears in a way it hadn't since Eliza came home with a bloody hand. I hardly heard what she said next, but I was glad I did, she seemed too smug to repeat herself. "What a shame on your family Mr. Thompson. An army man such as yourself, a devout catholic for a wife and a shameful Devil-child put upon ye. I can arrange for her to be transferred and told not to return to Tipperary again."

For the first time, I used my height and stature against a

woman. I pushed the evil little bitch to the side of the doorway with my shoulder and marched up the hall calling for Eileen. I headed upstairs, peering into rooms looking for a lunchroom or a dorm with my daughter sat in it, but instead found diabolical war-camp-like living conditions. When I saw the wooden beds with thin mattresses, I prayed to God she hadn't slept on one – if there's one thing the catholic church had its hand out for, it was money, so I saw no reason why the convent was so stuck for proper furnishings.

"Sir! This is a convent what are you doing–"

I had interrupted their precious prayer time.

"Ask her." I jerked my thumb at the nun running up the stairs behind me, blood-red in the face. As I continued up the hall tuning out their shouting and rules, I noticed the strongest smell – not that clean hospital smell you expect in a building full of pregnant women, but a detergent smell. Pushing open more doors, I found massive laundry rooms with women at all stages of pregnancy clearly overworking themselves. More nuns came towards me demanding to know my business, but I marched passed them, navigating through the steam. How could inhaling this be any good for anyone, let alone a pregnant woman.

"Eileen?" A few women stopped to stare and then jumped back to work when the flock of nuns followed me. I noticed one with a bruised cheek and a bandaged hand. So, the nuns were a dab hand at deciding how to deal with 'sinners' themselves, it seemed. "Eileen?"

"Dad? OH MY GOD, OH MY GOD, DAD!" Her long black hair had been harshly sheared up to her ears and she was in one of their work uniforms. As much as I wanted to hug her back while she clung to my waist, now was not the time.

"To your room, get your stuff. We are leaving." Holding onto my hand, she led me back through the convent, through the crowd of nuns. I was confused as to why she held onto me like a scared child in a crowd, but realised when a hand was raised to strike her.

"Back to work, whore." I caught the wrinkled, old wrist before it made contact.

"I will decide if my daughter needs to be disciplined, thank you." I focused on the back of Eileen's head, counting to ten to keep control of my temper as we rushed into her dorm and she gathered the one set of clothes she had. If I stopped to actually think, I would lose my temper, and having never done that on front of one of my children before, I did not want to scare one of my little girls—no matter how far she was in her pregnancy. We headed back down the stairs towards the ajar front door. I was glad she hadn't locked it—because I was not above lifting Eileen out a broken window.

"She is a child of God and she is a SINNER!" The screeching nuns followed me onto the front steps. The street was filling up with people headed to work. I turned to look down at the twelve or thirteen who had followed me.

"She is my daughter first. She is my responsibility. I don't know if you're aware, but this is Ireland, not the Vatican. We do not live by your laws and rules. We follow the government laws and rules and they do not say you own my daughter at all. I have respected the Catholic church for many years now. But that does not give you the right to make decisions for my family. On anything. Do not darken my doorstep again—whether I'm in Europe or at home. Because time and time again I will return and remind you ye are not the Gardaí, there were no broken laws and ye have no right to access my private property, let alone MY FUCKING CHILDREN. AM I CLEAR?" None of them answered, but none of them argued, so I expected they got the message.

"Up you hop, Eileen." I pulled the bike up; she stuffed her

clothes in the bucket and sat up on the handlebars. Every single person on the street and in the shops stood and stared shamelessly. As I headed back out the town, I spotted a faded 'Thompson & Family' sign at the bottom of the town before turning off. The relief of being home finally hit. I had my daughter back, now it was time for me to go home to my wife.

"Did you come home just for me, Dad?" Eileen sounded worn out. She stank of bleach and detergent.

"Yes, pet. I left the day I got Simon's letter." She was quiet for a few minutes. I noticed the slightest little baby bump.

"I hadn't even told anyone in the family yet. You should have seen Mam's face when the nun pushed past her and dragged me out by my hair. I should have told her, no one else."

"Simon's letter was started by your mother and covered in tears. She wants you back home, Eileen. I haven't been back yet, I came straight here to you, but I know straight up myself your mother and all ten siblings want you home."

"Thanks, Dad." Silence for another few minutes.

"And I know not one of us wants you to give up that baby, give up our family, or let some religious bats sell your baby off to America. I promise, pet. We're the Thompsons, we'll push on and figure it out." I got a kiss on the cheek for that one.

I met none of my children in town because they had moved back in with their mother after Eileen was taken, fearing she would have a heart attack. The front door was wide open, and I could hear young, squeaky voices playing games as I came up the road. The hedge grew tall over the wall since I'd left, so no one saw me stop the bike outside and help Eileen down. She swung the gate open drawing all attention to the front yard while I balanced the bike.

"EILEEN'S HERE!"

"Oh my God–"

"Oh, thank goodness! How did you get out?"

"Did you run away?" Bonnie asked Eileen, gazing up at her. No one noticed me standing in the gateway, all focused on their pregnant and tired sister.

"Not exactly." Eileen nodded towards me smiling, and all nine head swung around. I will never forget the shouting of 'Dad' and the feeling of being embraced by my children. But there was one person missing. Mary-Kate had been in the middle of the children holding Eileen's face, analysing her for illness or injury. She now stood holding her hand for support, gaping at me.

"Hello, darling." I smiled and walked up to her. Tears slowly built up in her eyes, and she threw herself at me with a force she hadn't since we were much, much younger. Murphy was right; she looked ill, but she also looked even more beautiful than the day I left her. My memory served her no justice.

"Joseph. You– I–"

She buried her head in my chest, unable to finish. God help me, it was going to kill me to walk away.

"I know, love. Me too." She didn't have to say anything, I knew what she was feeling. "I'm here for three days, we've got three more days together."

I looked up at our children. Some silently cried with her, others just stood in shock, watching their mother finally fall apart and hysterically cry, letting go in front of them for the first time.

14.

"It was awful, Joseph, them dragging her away, only the little ones at home and by the time I got word to Simon and Billy, they had her in there and wouldn't let anyone in. What were they supposed to do? Punch a nun in the face?" Mary-Kate had pulled her chair to the head of the table beside mine. She didn't seem to want to leave my side at all during my short stay, quite literally.

"They came fucking close to it," Billy huffed. Bonnie giggled and peeked up at him. During my absence, she started to cling to Billy and seemed quite comfortable plonking herself on his lap when we sat at the table.

"Tell me about it!" my wife huffed.

"Well, my mother and one of my big brothers locked up for attacking a member of the precious church would do me no good at all. Waiting for Dad was the right thing." Eileen held her mug out to Saoirse out for a refill of tea.

"So, what's your plan then?" Eliza snapped, glaring at her sister.

"I'm just home, Lizzie–"

"I don't care. You've a child on the way. You want to wear trousers and be all independent and a futuristic woman with all of your magazines and newspapers about women's rights and wanting to vote. Come on, Madam Future, what's the plan for the baby?" Just like that, the happy atmosphere dissolved around the temper of the eldest sister.

"I don't know if it's the whole bookkeeping and accounting in the shop that has you feel like head of the family or as if you're better than me, but you can be a right cruel bitch sometimes, Eliza."

"Is she allowed to talk to me like that, Mother?"

"Cop yourself on, Eliza. No need for this type of carry on. Dad's home for a few days. Everyone can be nice, or fuck off and let the rest of us enjoy it." Simon scowled at his sister. Looking around, I could see everyone closing their mouths—accepting Simon's word. It seemed he held sway in the family.

"I don't have a plan. I didn't want to be a single mother. I have a job, but I know it's not enough to support a child and to live, and even though I'm so glad I'm not staying in that convent to give birth—they had a point telling me that giving them up is probably the safest thing for them. But I don't need to be reminded of that every day either, Eliza." Unconsciously, she ran her hand over her little bump, just like her mother used to do when she was upset.

"We'll help, Eileen." Billy was the first to offer. "We all have jobs and there's enough of us that support you, that will help you out." He glanced at Eliza out of the corner of his eye. "Besides, you're fair smart. I reckon give ya ten years to let the baby grow up a bit and you'll train up in something fierce fancy and be able to manage everything yourself. There's nothing you've set your mind to that you haven't knocked out for the park yet." Eileen paled at hearing she could have to wait ten years to get going in the professional world, according to her brother.

"Yeah." Bonnie nodded vigorously in agreement.

"For the wedlock child? What life is that at all? Look at the comments we had about our dad being English, they'll suffer being the 'proddie' born out of wedlock! People are cruel, adults even more than children. Nothing will prepare them for it." Eliza looked just like her mother when she scowled.

"Forget it all for a second." I wanted Eileen to be totally honest with me when it came to being a mother. "When it comes to it, think of the child and yourself. Do you want to keep this baby?"

"Yes."

"Are you ready to be their mother?"

"No."

"Alright." I squeezed my wife's hand. Eleven children and twenty-one years of marriage, we didn't need words to talk. "Are you ready to be their sister?"

"What?"

"We always find a solution, dear." Mary-Kate smiled at her. "You feel giving them up is what's best, but don't want to really give them up; do both. Let your father and I adopt them. We'll raise them as your youngest brother or sister. You get to keep them, but you don't have to worry about them or how to raise them. Because they will be our youngest child."

Eileen had tears in her eyes which made me start to panic.

"Think it over darling—"

"Yes. I'll let you adopt them. Oh, thank you so much, I'll help out and contribute and everything, I promise." She hugged her mother and kissed me on the cheek.

"So, Eileen's baby is now Mammy and Daddy's baby?" Thomas asked.

"Yes, Tommy," Eliza stood up, "it happens when silly people make bad decisions that affect poor little babies. It's called jumping through hoops." She walked out. I couldn't help but think how she had a temper on her that would have made my father-in-law proud.

"Ah here, if she doesn't cop on—"

"Leave it, Billy," Mary-Kate scolded him, causing him to

throw his hands up. "Eliza is trying to protect Eileen in her own way, it just happens to be a bit cruel. She means well. Adopting the baby saves the baby prejudice. Eliza wants to save Eileen from any hardship in the world, all of ye for that matter. She's just not great at expressing herself."

"Her inability to express herself will get her a thumping someday, if she can't have basic fucking manners," Saoirse muttered.

"Adult or not, you'll still get a smack of a tea towel if you don't start behaving. All of ye!" Mary-Kate stood to start getting dinner ready and Eileen plonked into her chair, kissing me on the cheek again.

"I mean it, Dad. Thank you."

Much to the surprise of everyone that was sitting at that table who heard Eliza's harsh words, but as expected by Mary-Kate and I, I got a letter five months later telling me Eliza was with Eileen all throughout her early, yet long, labour and insisted on being the first to hold the baby. She was also the first to march up the aisle of the church in the middle of a Sunday service and chastise the priest for refusing to christen the newest Thompson baby, because he saw Eileen with a bump, not Mary-Kate. Most of my children were happy to no longer have to attend services when Mary-Kate was informed they were no longer welcome. To my surprise, I had to write Hazel quite a large letter explaining her she didn't need to go to church to pray to God for me to come home and be safe.

A copy of the adoption cert came after that, stating that I was, for the last time, a father. My youngest son—Theodore.

Christmas 1945

Had I not gone home for one week and seen my children that little bit older and their personalities a little bit more defined, I would have gotten an awful shock returning when the second world war ended. I had not seen John in the almost-six years, and he looked entirely different. Eileen's little bump was now my raging toddler with bright, orange hair. Bonnie, to my horror, was wearing a very pale-pink rouge (it was all Mary-Kate could talk her down to). Tommy played for the local hurling team, and Billy finally had a job that he wasn't fired from within the first two weeks.

"You're some twat, Billy." John's fiancé, Sandra, was laughing at him scraping icing off the floor and out of his hair. That too—I also had an in-law waiting for me to come home to finally get married.

"When God was handing out brains, Billy was hiding behind the door,"

"Ah, shut up, ye lot. Look, only Bonnie is nice enough to help me out. Ye're all rotting in Hell. Thank you, Bon."

I missed the jokes and slagging a lot more than I had realised. Just to sit here and listen was such a blessing to me now. Coming home this time was a lot different to coming home to my parents. While there was no sense of grief or loss like back then, my children had grown up and changed a lot without me. My parents had the same faces and the same personalities when I came home to them. Now it felt like my wife was the only thing the same, and I had to get to know them all again.

"Morning, all. Merry Christmas!" Saoirse stumbled in the door with a literal sack of gifts.

"I hope they were bought." Billy had decided to sit on the

floor—hiding the icing in case of his mother's return from the kitchen. "Just cause you're a wizard with a sewing machine, doesn't mean you should get to cheap out on presents"

"You're decked out head to toe in my free clothing right now. Be nice or you can start buying again." She left the duty of dishing out to Tommy and Bonnie, everything perfectly wrapped and labelled. She sat on the arm of my chair. "Dad, I spoke to Eileen on the telephone in my neighbours earlier. She knows it's your first Christmas home, but she thinks it will be better to really let Theo grow up a bit and not resemble a baby at all before seeing him. She'll call down next week and stay with me, though, so you can call over." I nodded and patted her knee.

"I know, dear, it's alright. She's doing well in Dublin?"

"Fantastic."

"That brings me buckets of joy." I stood up to join Mary-Kate in the kitchen. My knees and ankles felt as though they were on fire, and I stumbled my first few steps.

"You alright, Dad?" Anthony stood to help me, but I pulled away.

"Grand, son. Just sat for too long I think." In the kitchen, Mary-Kate was dividing veg between an enormous number of plates. She prepared and cooked it all, insisting she could do it alone, but I think they are all big enough to dish up their own.

"Dinner's done!" I called into the hall, "Come and grab what you want. It's self-serve."

"Joseph." Mary-Kate scolded me. She had a slight tremble to her hands. I wonder if she had gone to the doctor yet.

"What? You're always cooking or cleaning and giving out to me for trying to help. They can get their own carrots." She pecked me on the lips.

"Eeeeeeeeeeeeew!" Tommy was first to run in Billy behind

him, imitating him.

"I didn't miss that!" Billy made a face at Tommy.

The first of the New Year, Hazel came skipping through the front door, quite literally, with the announcement she had secured herself her first job. She would be working, part-time, in a manor house owned by some posh English widow, cleaning and learning to cook. I thought she was too young to be getting a job as she was still a teenager, but she gave me this huge 'young woman' speech that would have made Eileen proud.

"They don't realise how much you've missed out on, how much they changed in six years," Mary-Kate whispered in my ear. She couldn't be right; if it wasn't for Theo, I would spend every minute following Mary-Kate around for company. Our house was empty by the time I woke up, and my children passed through so quickly in the evenings I hardly got to properly talk to them.

The first week of her employment, Hazel pranced in the door in the uniform provided to her by the house staff, including a pair of shiny black shoes. Her older siblings thought she was being too big for her boots because she was the first in the family with a job that got her a uniform not made by her family. Mary-Kate was quick to remind them how big their heads were when they all got their first jobs, and to be a little more considerate of the younger one's pride.

Her airs and graces disappeared not even a month in, when five minutes after she left for work, she ran back in the back door screeching so loud Theo dropped his beaker and I dropped my tea.

"DAD!" She collapsed into the chair beside me, face completely white, hands shaking. "He's after me—I thought I saw him standing there yesterday, but how could he, so it must have been my mind playing tricks, but today he ran at me. HE RAN AT ME DAD!" She was gripping my arm so tight her knuckles were white.

"Who's running?" Billy was coming in the front door with his mother. "Jaysus, what happened to you? Shouldn't you be galivanting around that big house with your fancy job?"

"Hazel, what happened?" Parent instinct kicked in and, like me, Mary-Kate picked up on Hazel's very real fear.

"He was hiding in the woods yesterday, standing and staring. But today he chased me all the way back home!" Theo looked up at me mouth agape and milk running down his chin, looking as confused as I was.

"Some lad is chasing you?" Billy, who had recently taken up bare-knuckle boxing, sat up all tense and ready for a fight.

"Not 'some lad', Billy" Hazel glanced over her shoulder at the door and out the kitchen window, as if the offending man was going to be there watching her. "Tadgh Shannon." Billy let out a rip of a laugh so loud, Theo jumped for the second time.

"The IRA soldier shot in the back running away from the manor house fifty, almost sixty, years ago?" Mary-Kate asked and looked at me so puzzled I almost joined Billy and laughed at the look on her face.

"YES!" Hazel nodded her head so vigorously her hair started falling out of its bun. It was a strange situation, and I still had no idea what was going on, but she seemed utterly convinced and still very afraid. "He has that suit on—the long dress jacket all shaggy and green so he can hide in the grass!" I frowned and looked back at Mary-Kate. Our daughter had no reason to know what a green turncoat looked like—so someone must be wearing it.

"Billy, walk your sister to work the long way by the road. I'll go through the grove with you tomorrow and sort this out." I gave my son a sharp look to cut off whatever smart comment he was going to pass. Half grumbling, half giggling to himself, he led her out the front door.

"What is going on, Joseph?" Mary-Kate picked up Theo's beaker to refill it, and I threw the tea towel down to soak up the mess we had made.

"It'll all be sorted tomorrow, darling."

"You walk ahead of me, I'll only be a few paces behind, if they see me coming, they won't try and scare you and we won't sort this." Hazel scowled and bit her cheek. "I promise, poppet, I won't let anyone get you. Now you go on ahead, and don't glance back at me." She looked me up and down before striding off, clearly worried by how much I was limping. I could admit I wasn't in the best shape; time and age had not been kind to the ailments I got in the trenches—a second war had done them even worse. But, if motivated by one of my girls being attacked, I was betting on myself to win that fight. I had no injury a little adrenaline couldn't fix.

Hazel headed off through the grove, about ten paces ahead of me and so tense her shoulders practically touched her ears. I did my best to step quietly glancing around her for someone behind a tree. Lo and behold, she wasn't even quarter of the way through the grove when a tall figure in a green turncoat stepped out behind a massive tree. He was turned ever so slightly, so he was also looking at Hazel from behind, but far left enough to be in her peripheral vision. Screeching so load, she put barn owls to shame; Hazel ran back to me, veering off to the right to put space between her and her stalker. His costume let him down, the undergrowth dangling over his eyes shielded me until my daughter was by my side and he was already coming in our direction. He, himself, had closed the distance between us, before he saw me waiting for him.

Turning, he ran—well, attempted to. He had a heavy limp on his right leg, both slowing him down and identifying him. I had no reason to run after him. Old Paddy Cleary, with his gammy knee from a farm injury, had limped on his left leg into Murphy's pub for many years. He also had IRA heritage in his family that he bragged about when he had too many whiskeys.

"Who is it, Dad?" Hazel had gripped my hand with both of hers, as if she was only a child again.

"A guy from the pub. Around my age, I think. No worries though, poppet. You continue on to work now and I'll go visit him." I pecked her on the forehead and watched her walk away until she disappeared out the other side of the trees.

The back door nearly came off the hinges when I banged it shut behind me. Theo spun in his chair and I ruffled his hair to keep him calm.

"Joseph?" Mary-Kate stuck her head out the sitting room.

"Paddy Cleary. He is terrorizing my girl." I was practically snarling at my wife thinking about it.

"Why—Joseph what *are* you doing?" Mary-Kate followed me to our room, where I was hunched over at our wardrobe.

"Going to pay him a visit. Where is that stick Billy got me

as a joke for Christmas—I'll be needing it." I got no answer but
didn't think much of it. The stick had fallen across the back of
the wardrobe, and I had to bend my knees down to reach in for
it. It took me a minute to fully straighten up, but when I did, anger
took the wheel again and I marched to the front door—it was
locked. The spare key from the top of the door jamb was gone
too.

"Why is the door locked?" I stomped into the kitchen, where
again, the back door was locked and the spare key missing.

"You are not going anywhere in that temper." Mary-Kate
was in front of the stove, arms crossed across her chest, adamant.

"Let me out now, that old creep needs to be taught a lesson!
Following my girl around the woods, scaring her. What would he
do if he caught her, eh?" Theo started to cry at my shouting.

"Cleary is stupid, but not enough to hurt her. The old fool
probably just thought it was funny. Besides, he's the same age as
you, Joseph, even if she tripped, he wouldn't catch up. You will
not beat the shit out of him with a stick for being a twat. You will
stay in here until you can control your temper!" She picked Theo
up and marched into the sitting room, cooing to him. I looked
around the kitchen, exasperated, no idea where to start looking.

"Mary-Kate, open that door now!" I followed her. She put
Theo in front of the radio and turned to me, now furious herself.

"I'll take it kindly you watch how you talk to me. The last
time you yelled at me it ended in tears, but I was a girl—this time,
you will run off crying. Don't push me, Joseph Thompson." She
came right up to me, poking me in the stomach with her tiny fist
clenched.

"Darling, remember how I lost my temper then because the
poppies reminded me of my brothers." Her gaze softened
momentarily before resuming its glare. "Well, firstly, that creep

is dressing up as a soldier who was killed when his back was turned. Secondly, he is terrorizing one of my girls—which no father would take. And lastly, he is getting enjoyment out of making someone scream from terror—you know where I'm used to hearing those screams? Well, now one of those horrific screams is coming out of my little girl. Let Me. Out." She stepped back, calming down from her own temper.

"Look, I will go and deliver the message to him—and make your points clear. But you are staying put. I've just gotten you back you will not be spending time in the local clinker and face assault charges." I opened my mouth to argue, but she snapped the stick off me and silenced me with a ferocious glare. "That is my compromise, Joseph. That is final. I'll unlock the doors when you've calmed down—and I can read you like a book, so don't try pretending." She headed to our room to return my walking stick to its home.

"Fine, but you've to give him that look you just gave me the entire time you're talking to him. And I get to stare him down at the pub and set a drunk Billy on him!"

15.

Despite showing I could stamp around the place when motivated, my wife let me do very little on account of my knees and feet. I couldn't hide that the pains I had anymore, and it was hard for me to move about on frosty mornings, so she decided I shouldn't do much. While it was a delight to be back with my wife and children, trying to sleep was the hardest part of the day and the one person who saw that every night was Mary-Kate.

It was even harder to sit still and watch her run around like a headless chicken after teenagers. I kept Theo with me most of the time, sitting in my chair in the mornings and going off on little walks with him when I could move easier after lunch. But Bonnie, Thomas and Anthony seemed to be very accustomed to having their mother do lots of things for them; practically everything. I had to give credit to my older children, yes even Billy; when they were old enough, they cleaned up their own dishes, washed their own clothes and moved out where they looked after themselves. The younger ones did not seem to have that initiative, and despite my hints and suggestions, they still didn't get the point.

"Where's your mother?" Anthony and Thomas stayed staring at the television set.

"She's outside washing clothes." Bonnie was causing some strong petrol stench with a nail polish.

"Really? None of you offered to do it today?" No answer. "Anthony, what month is it?"

"Uh, February." He still couldn't look at me when he spoke.

"Thomas, what day is today?" Thomas had the manners to actually look at me and then picked up the paper off the armchair.

"It iiis—Oh no." He turned off the television.

"Tommy! I was watching that–"

"It's Mam's birthday"

"Are you kidding me!?" Bonnie slammed the little bottle on the table. "HAZEL!" Hazel stuck her head round the door. "Why didn't you remind us?"

"Because I have to remind ye every year, ye always take my gift ideas and I think one year of shame and embarrassment and ye'll never forget her birthday again." She shrugged. "Besides. If ye were nice enough people, ye would just know."

"That is so shit of you." Anthony shook his head.

"Hang on, you came out of the kitchen, I bet you're using the morning to bake her something while she's not inside—let's pretend we all made it." Thomas pointed at Hazel with the newspaper.

"Good thinking, Tommy," Bonnie smiled, "that's way she won't be upset that we forgot. Personally, Hazel, I think you want the attention of being the only one still living at home to give her something and it would just break her heart if us three did nothing."

"Ahem, get out." I decided to contribute to the argument.

"Yeah, that sort of slyness isn't a part of this family, Hazel, Thompson's help each other out. Go back to our cake and finish decorating it before she gets back." Thomas flapped his hands in the air, herding Hazel back.

"I was talking to you three, actually." Three jaws hung open. "You should all be ashamed of yourselves. Granted, you've told me your mother needed to be busy while I was gone, she got upset when she had nothing to do. But I left thinking I had

140

children who would help her, or sit in the kitchen and chat to her, or step up when they were old enough to do their own stuff. I am so disappointed. Since I got back, it's become *very* clear you three are used to being served and waited on. So, you three get ye're asses up and walk into town, like my parents, myself, your mother and older siblings would do when we needed something, and go buy her something with all that pocket money all ye're siblings constantly give ye, so ye three aren't the only ones without gifts after Hazel and Theo give her theirs. Tonight, I'll take her into town for dinner and when I come home, I want to see the chores divided up between ye—and not just for today, for *every* day. Understood?"

They nodded and left, passing a very smug Hazel who stared them all in the eye as they passed.

"You really making a cake?"

"Yup."

"Any offcuts?"

"Yup, come on."

"Ooooh, chocolate cake for brekkie, eh?" I poked Theo in the belly, making him giggle. When I had him sat up in the middle of the table with a bowl, I went out the back to Mary-Kate. Hazel was responsible enough not to let him roll off.

She was sitting up on her knees next to a huge basin of steamy water and four empty buckets from where she had walked to the well to fill the basin, and was scrubbing a stain out of one of the boys' shirts. She had tied her shawl to her to stop it sliding off, and I could see her breath in the frosty weather. She heard me coming and quickly glanced back.

"Go back inside, Joseph. I know ya won't admit the cold bothers you, but I know it does. Off ya pop."

"Leave them there." I grabbed her by the elbows and pulled

141

her up, "Thomas and Anthony have volunteered to finish that since it's your birthday and they're their clothes. They'll do it in the afternoon when it's warmed up a bit."

"Hah, I know they forgot my birthday. Those three always sponge off of Hazel and they think I don't know. I'm their mother, of course I do. I also know you and you've decided they'll do this. Well, I'm not leaving these to soak all day and not be done, and I'd rather do them myself properly."

"No." She could turn back to it all she wanted, I was still bigger and stronger 'up and inside'. I grabbed her hands to pull her towards the back door. Despite being in warm water, they were freezing cold and looked really sore. "Huh, well you're heading down to the doctor tomorrow to get some cream or something for them."

"I have the pub shift tomorrow night; I can't go with my hands all wrapped up or creamy. I'll drop a pint into someone's lap." I stopped and looked down at her.

"I know I can't help as much anymore, but the kids can step up and look after their share. I think we should go back to our bit of normal before the war. I can't do as much, but I could help the girls in the shop in the mornings with Theo so you have time to yourself, and we could have Friday pub dinner. You should spend more time with your friends, and I'd like to spend time with our children again. We could even head up to Dublin for a weekend before the wedding and meet our future in-laws."

She bit her lip and frowned. There was one ever so small line sticking where she did that while she thought.

"I just – I'm in the habit so that I don't sit and worry, and now it's over I don't know what to do because I was so closed off to friends, and even my own children, for so long. It sounds nice, though. Just a case of finding a new routine." I kissed her forehead.

"Exactly. We only technically have one child in the house now. The others are old enough to do their bit like all the older ones did. I hope I don't end up in the doghouse with this, but maybe we should enjoy being a bit... old, now." I whispered the last part and braced myself. I got an elbow in the ribs as I expected—something I strangely missed. "Also, for you, my love. Happy Birthday." I handed her the small box I had in my cardigan pocket.

"*Joseph.*" She scowled up at me as she undid the ribbon. "You know how I feel about expensive gifts—don't lie! I know jewellery is expensive." She opened the little box and gasped at the gold ring with little diamonds running across the band.

"It's an eternity ring," I said, "never heard of the concept, but I was with lads my age out there and they were talking about giving their wives eternity rings before they left or saving for one when they went home. It should be for our anniversary, but I couldn't wait until August to give it to you." I took it out and slid it on her ring finger, finishing the trio—engagement, wedding and eternity.

"I love it." It was nice to see her cry from happiness again.

"Good. To make it sit a bit more comfortably, how about getting the doctor to fix up all those sores?"

"How about a compromise? I'll go for my hands, and you come for your legs."

"Alright, fine." I huffed and rolled my eyes, imitating Bonnie, earning a laugh. "Now let's go have some tea."

Settling her, I passed her a mug of tea and a big slice of Hazel's cake. I warmed some milk for Theo—the back door was old and letting cold into the kitchen; I would have to fix that.

"I hadn't seen that in a while," Hazel muttered, washing up

some dishes.

"What?"

"Mam, laughing and smiling. And still having a smile on her face more than five minutes later." I wrapped my arm around her shoulder, giving her a little side hug.

"Well, we're gonna work on that from now on. Be a bit less shell-shocked together."

I turned to look at her sitting with Theo on her lap, letting him have the odd bite of her cake, not caring he had already had a quite a lot of it. I was looking forward to the growing old part of our lives happening. She caught my eye and smiled that cheeky smile where her eyes twinkle, the one I got outside Murphy's all those years ago when she was wrapped in daisies.

16.

March 1966

Old age suited me much more than Mary-Kate. I was used to limitations and pains from the first war. Mary-Kate was not used to struggling to get out of bed, hurting more on cold mornings and taking longer to do simple things. She insisted on continuing as she had in her thirties and forties, looking after our adult children too much and always finding something to fix. For the most part, much to my children's complaint, I let her. I knew her longer than any of them and I knew better than to try and suggest she was too old for anything. They saw their aging frail mother who had always fixed their bumps and bruises and gone out of her way to help them, not the little barmaid I knew that could give as good as she got. Getting out of a bed four feet off the ground hurt enough; I did not want to try it after spending a night on the pancake-flat settee for suggesting she was too old to do something anymore.

That all came to a halt when she flew off her high nelly on the way to town and into a dyke full of nettles. The pedals removed the first few layers of skin on her shins, she fractured her left wrist and was roasted all down one side.

"It's enough now, Dad, she won't listen to us, it's your turn," Eileen scolded me in the kitchen. She was standing in front of the sink, arms crossed, glaring at me. She looked so like her mother when she was barking orders.

"I know, darling, I will. But I can't go in all guns blazing like ye have. She won't listen. There's a way of talking to your mother, all right?"

"Well talk to her before she gets herself killed flying around the place. Old age is making her cranky and impossible to talk to!"

"Enough of that now, Eileen."

"Well, it is—"

"Enough! She's your mother and there's no need to talk of her like that! She's done plenty for you and all your siblings, a bit of respect now." She bit the inside of her cheek to stop snapping back at me, but she did stay quiet. "Ye can't sort things out with her cause half of ye *have* her short temper and ye just butt heads. I don't know if you've noticed, but we live in the middle of nowhere—if we take her mode of transport she'll just walk everywhere, rain, hail or snow. We can't just give up our lives and stay home all the time. You're married now, Eileen, would you fancy years of just the two of you in an empty house? She needs her afternoon teas and meetings and community... *Things,* to keep her happy, and me entertained with all the stories. You can't tell her 'You're old now, you stay at home all the time'." Silence for a few minutes.

"Didn't think of it like that." She sat at the table; temper gone now.

"Dad? Dr. Sullivan sent this cream for Mam's face– oh, hi Eileen." Theo had arrived home from school already.

"Drop it into her, Theo, she's resting in bed." She nodded to our room door. When he left, she leaned closer to whisper, "Simon said he had an idea instead of the bike. A retirement present for Mam from the pub and, being honest, for you finishing at the shop for good. I wasn't sure because I feel it's more work for ye, but they insist ye'll be happy. You're pushing seventy, and Mams not too far behind ya."

"Alright, what's the idea?"

"Well, if you agree about the shop, it's for you too. I don't want to spoil it." I nodded, happy to forget it, but she had a guilty look about her.

"What?"

"Well, see, Simon told me… but it might be Billy's idea." I laughed.

"Oh. Oh no! Not happening! Forget it." I stood up to refill the pot for more tea.

"Well, to be fair to him, he's copped on an awful lot since he got married! And even Eliza said it was a good idea. He's surprised all of us. I, personally, think it was Kitty's idea and he's stealing it, laying claim."

"Forget trying to justify that looders fancy ideas. Want me to believe it's smart, I'll believe it when I see it. I'll talk your mother down for ye, after we see this amazing surprise. I raised that fool; I know what happens when he gets… creative" I shook my head. Eileen had a soft spot for Billy because he helped out a lot with paying for Theo's schooling—she could no longer be trusted when it came to finding out what stupid endeavour he was on, because she felt she should give him a chance.

"Who's getting creative?" Theo was back and ransacking the cupboards again.

"Billy," I whispered dramatically.

"Uh-oh. Don't tell Mam, she's had enough of a bad week, we don't want her to have a heart attack." He started trying to make a sandwich, making holes in the bread with the butter knife. Despite being smart enough to know when his brothers were being daft, Theo had his own little ways of showing he wasn't the brightest spark too. He had brains for books, but not for basic life skills.

"There's gonna be a pound of butter *in* that slice of bread, Theo."

"Yeah, I can see that—and Mam's not big on butter, is she?"

"Ah here, I'll make her one. You can have that little butter ball." I took the loaf off of him and couldn't believe how happily he ate it. The kid also had a stomach of a terrier.

"Eileen was with you for a good while, today." Mary-Kate looked at me suspiciously over her cup of water. "I'm not giving away that bike, Joseph."

"And I told her that, love." The glare turned into a smile.

"Good, I knew you were smarter than to go up against me too." She pecked me on the cheek. She had never been seriously hurt before, the odd mild burn from the stove, but nothing serious. It killed me seeing her wrist all bandaged up and her face all blistered.

"Well, enjoy your bed rest. We're walking to Murphy's for your retirement Saturday evening."

"I told them I don't like fuss!" She banged one clenched fist down onto her lap, temper rising.

"I know, love, but they love you very dearly and want to do something nice for you, that's all." Playing the 'they-love-you' card always calmed her down.

"Oh, well then it's grand, I suppose." She slowly shuffled down into bed.

"Goodnight, speedy." Her reply was just a sharp elbow into my ribs.

That weekend, I had to admit they had done well. They had gotten the usual punters in, Mary-Kate's friends and their husbands and some of the neighbours into the pub. Some brought baked goods and there was extra help in the kitchen for finger food. Saoirse even got some of our regulars at the shop out to the village for the event. I had actually happily given up the shop. Every joint crippled me now, and using the sewing machine or even just pinning hurt like hell.

"Anthony has just gotten here! Ye're present is outside!" Bonnie ran up to our booth, practically bouncing.

"Why couldn't we have gotten it at home?" Mary-Kate was entirely suspicious of them all.

"And why is it outside? Is it something we can't have inside?" I was with her on it. They had gradually come home from all over the country, John and Sandra from Dublin, Bonnie and Hazel from Galway, Thomas up from Kerry. All week, they had being giving each other secretive looks, whispering and laughing. Bonnie caught us by our hands, pulling us up slowly.

"Just come on! The surprise is part of the fun!"

"Hmph," Mary-Kate started muttering to herself, "maybe for your generation, but not ours!"

I almost apologised to Billy when I walked out the pub and saw the brand-new cart and the young donkey with a little bow on her harness.

"SURPRISE!" They were gathered around it. Bonnie hopped up into it with Eliza and Saoirse.

"We haven't named her yet—thought you'd like to do that, Mam!" Billy was on the far side of the donkey petting her ears.

"I—Oh my God! That's so expensive!" Mary-Kate had her hands over her mouth in complete shock.

"We all chipped in, so no it wasn't. Simon dropped off a load of meal and a trough to the home place, just after ye left." John was the voice of reason, and probably the one who stopped his brothers painting the cart multicolour or something ridiculous.

"Now ye can spin around anywhere without any effort!" Eliza got out of the cart, pulling Bonnie down with her.

"Without injury," Billy added.

"So, any chance I can have that bike now, Mam?" Eileen braced herself for a scolding. Mary-Kate laughed.

"Well, I suppose so." They all stared clapping and high fiving each other over their first ever victory against their mother. "Oh, this evening couldn't get any better, ye did so well." I passed her my hankie and we climbed up to sit in it for the first time.

"Actually, it could!" Kitty and Sandra, Billy and John's wives came out the pub behind us. Sandra introduced Kitty to Billy when he visited them two years ago, and the two always stayed in contact after Kitty moved down here. They had tears in their eyes and the biggest smiles on their faces.

"We're pregnant!" They yelled it together, John running to Sandra and Billy, running around Kitty jumping in circles.

"Dr. Sullivan confirmed for us there now because he couldn't get the message to us with all the party planning." Kitty wiped her tears while Hazel and Bonnie sandwiched her in a hug.

"Hey, ye're first grandchildren." Theo beamed up at us, delighted at the thought of being an uncle. Eileen gulped and glanced to Mary-Kate and I. Mary-Kate smiled up at me, tears in her eyes again.

"I'll finally be a granny!" Eileen relaxed. She was grateful, but always wary of how we felt about Theo being our son now that she was around for good again.

After starting the week off with injury and panic, we finish edit with a lot of laughs, old friends and news of become grandparents for the first time.

February 1970

"I'M TELLING GRANDAD!" The high-pitched screeching made me wince now.

"I'M TELLING FIRST!" Theo, acting like the child, ran into the sitting room, grinning at me. Tyler, doing his best to catch up with his little steps, huffed around the corner after him, wide eyed and pointing at him.

"He pushed me, he pushed me!"

"I pushed you 'cause little messers deserve to get pushed." Theo poked him in the belly, making him panic more.

"Enough now," Mary-Kate called from the kitchen. "Theo come strain these spuds for me and stop harassing the poor child." In true thirty-year-old fashion, Theo stuck his tongue out at Tyler.

"Don't tell your mother I told you this, but if someone pushes you over, get up and push them back." I held the biscuit tin out to him and winked, getting a smile back. Temper tantrum fully avoided. I wouldn't say it out loud for fear of upsetting people, but where my kids were let play and fight and learn stuff themselves, they had become these parents that stopped fights and gave time outs and punishments. Personally, I think if you hit your brother and get a black eye in return, that's punishment enough. But it was a new generation, and I kept my thoughts to myself. The day Kitty awarded Tyler with putting his dish to the sink with a lollipop, Mary-Kate was almost caught rolling her eyes at me.

"Right, come on you and we get you home to your Mammy." Theo came back swiping a biscuit. "I'll be up in the morning with ye're turf." I nodded and saluted him, and he headed off with Tyler, waving back at me.

"SHUT THE DOOR—ah, here." Mary-Kate stomped up the hallway and slammed it shut behind them.

"Just because he's fully grown doesn't mean the whack of a tea towel won't help him to remember, love." She joined me on the setee, slightly out of breath from storming, heading up the hall. Much to her own disappointment, Mary-Kate didn't go far very fast and when she did, she had to sit down to catch her breath.

"He's not the only one, they all leave it wide open. And I don't think I have it in me to go back get the tea towel and catch up with any of them anyway"

"You and me both" that got a smile.

September 1970

"CLOSE THE DOOR!" Simon flew out the gate in a rush off to make it to the pub to see the match. Mary-Kate stomped up the hall muttering to herself and swearing at him under her breath.

"I don't see why they all insist on buying us turf and complaining of the cold in this house if they leave the door open all the time." Back up to the kitchen to the screaming the pot.

"I came out the bathroom and that ass was halfway in the hallway." I heaved myself up, heading out for my mug and toast.

"Exactly! And her name is Jackie; have the respect to call her by her name." Only my Mary-Kate would have a soft spot for a donkey. "That reminds me, Bonnie will be down early in the morning for the train station."

"Ah, that." I made a face into my mug of tea.

"Yes that! The appointment is for good reason. You wouldn't have been referred if it wasn't serious." My plate of jam toast flew at ninety down the table at me. Ah, so she was in a bickering form. "You're on the two walking sticks anyway, Joseph, if they go through with it, when you recover it will still just be two sticks and no pain." She sat beside me, green eyes burning out from the loose grey hair that had fallen from her bun.

"Sir, yes, sir." I saluted her with my index finger, as if she was a commanding officer. The fight melted into that young, twenty-year-old smile. I got a light whack on the shoulder and a bemused, "Joseph."

17.

"Mammy, I can do that!" Bonnie had her hands on her hips giving out to her mother. For someone upset, her mother got out of bed early to hitch the cart to the donkey; she was doing a better job of spectating than helping. Granted she was four months pregnant, but don't whine if you won't or can't help. "Dad, tell her stop."

"Tried already. She took one of my sticks off me and whacked me with it."

"Right, all done. Careful with her, don't be too strict. Mind your father. Joseph don't let her get notions wandering around Cork city." Instructions were dealt, and kisses were planted on cheeks. "See you this evening with your tea."

"Will admitting I was wrong help by any chance?" I tried to dig myself out of the hole.

The traffic in Cork city in a morning was madness, and I insisted we hop out the taxi a block from the hospital and walk the last bit to be on time. We were now lost.

"Nope. We are not lost, we are misplaced. We need not worry. Once you have a mouth, you have a map!" Bonnie scanned the crowd, picking who she would ask.

"What criteria are you looking for! Just ask someone!" I

didn't want to admit it, but being seaside, Cork was bloody cold and my feet were starting to burn again.

"People can lie, Dad, it's not like 'the old days'." She rolled her eyes at me. "Especially anyone under twenty, little brats. A Garda would be handy or a mammy, 'cause they think of their kids being lost and want to help. But I can't see either. I'll nip into that shop over there; if they lie, they know I can go back and complain so they've something to lose." I got her mother's wicked grin and she took off. Standing there glancing around, I wondered how people lived in *this*. No quiet, no peace, no easy strolls.

"What's the verdict so?" Simon walked to the train station to drive the cart home for us after work.

"All ten amputated, but the actual foot is fine." Hearing my kids discuss my health and treatment bothered me. I didn't like the roles being reversed between parent and child.

"Right, we'll move in so."

"Excuse me?" I stopped sulking at Simon's sudden announcement.

"Myself and Eileen will move in when you're first home to help you and Mammy until you're back on your feet. No arguing, we both know Mam will go super-mammy looking after you, and potentially hurt herself if you're down." I couldn't argue. It would be Mary-Kate to decide to retile the roof while I was in a wheelchair.

Back at home, Mary-Kate fought tooth and nail not to be babysat for two months. She tried to barter letting Simon and Billy put in that electricity and a telephone, but instead they told her that was being done regardless of surgeries, no arguing. When they left that night, I half laughed at her.

"You can't be that mad at them."

155

"And why not?"

"Mary-Kate, in all honesty, darling, where do you think they learned to be so stubborn from?" She shrugged and pulled herself out of the setee slowly. "When did you start having back problems?" She looked a little guilty.

"Saoirse marched out and left the door open and, in a rage, I twisted funny standing up and now I can't lean forwards. When you were in the kitchen with Simon, Bonnie had to unlace my boots for me, so I can kick them off before hopping into bed." I was no longer the only patient in the house. After a night of thinking about it, I had Theo use our telephone for me to order the solution to Mary-Kate's problem.

"Still, it's fucking stupid!" Hazel was bickering with her siblings over a game of snakes and ladders. She had beat everyone to spot ninety-nine four times in one game, only to be sent down that big snake to spot four each time.

"Hello?" I peered out the window. He was here just a week after the call; perfect timing.

"Who is that?" Mary-Kate elbowed me.

"A mechanic. Son of a lad, a worker on the railway back when I met you." I heaved myself up from my wheelchair and hobbled out.

"What does he want a mechanic for?" I took my package, he refused payment based off the stories his dad had told him and we chatted for ten minutes. I left the box into our room on Mary-Kate's dresser. I would install it when they were all gone home.

"You're some fucking loser! Loser!" Billy was leaning over the sink, jeering at Hazel out the small kitchen window."

"Her temper is gonna get her hurt!" Bonnie wagged her finger at me from the end of the table as if whatever happened was my fault. Mary-Kate was in my chair, holding a hankie to her mouth trying to hide her laugher, but not at all hiding the tears running down her face. Joining Billy at the sink, I could see Hazel sitting on the turf with one of those long 'movie-star' cigarettes she loved, a gallon of petrol used for fire starting at her feet, and the snakes and ladders board game four feet away from her, on fire.

"She could have lit it a bit further away from the turf."

"That's all you've to say, Dad? She set it on fire, and you're concerned about where." Billy was all disgusted which was rather ironic.

"Glass houses, Billy, glass houses."

"Here's the first one." Mary-Kate loved my little adjustment to the front door, and was waiting for its first victim on a kitchen chair in the hallway. Simon struggled with the door and eventually used his body weight to slide through it.

"What the fuck is that?" He pointed at the door, looking disgusted.

"A tractor spring." One part attached to the wall, one to the door. It might be difficult to open, but it snapped shut with a fabulous bang.

"You're gone mad on them fucking pain killers. There'll be others with missing toes because of you."

"Well ye should have shut the door before your mother threw her back out following ye around like she did when ye were five." I smiled up at him.

July 1973

"So, how do I get it out the door?" Kitty looked between Mary-Kate and me. I shrugged.

"After you said you wanted it, it was no longer my problem." I got an exasperated look.

"Go out the back door maybe?" Mary-Kate put her left-laced foot down and her right one up on the little stool. Saoirse moved in a year ago to help because between the two of us, we couldn't master much without help.

"Well, can I prune the blackcurrant bush back, so I don't look like one of those characters from the horror films that do be in the pictures?"

"Say no, Dad," Saoirse whispered dramatically, "I want to see her pushing her way through, thorns in that lovely red hair."

"Hey, no way. You're taking the other side of it! It's only fair!" Kitty's hands went to her hips. The law had been laid now. Mary-Kate was giving her mother's old dresser to Kitty for her and Billy's new house. He was now working on a stud farm and had gotten help getting on the list for a new build locally. Mary-Kate had given ornaments and old keepsakes to every one of the children, but still there were some jealous whispers that an in-law got the dresser. I knew well it was, because Billy's house was the closest and Mary-Kate was afraid of moving it too far.

Bits of furniture and machinery, like my old sewing machine, had begun moving out of the house this year both because of lack of use and to make space for four struggling legs and four walking sticks. The only room in the house that didn't have wide spaces for old people hobbling was the children's old room—Saoirse's room now.

"Well, screw ye making fun of me, I'm going getting hedge clippers," and she was off marching out the back.

"This I have to see." Saoirse was off to wind her up. Kitty was a great help around the house for us, and she would try to do anything to help us out—but she wasn't the most coordinated.

"Well, don't leave the clippings everywhere, John and Sandra are bringing the kids down for a week–" Mary-Kate leaned over the setee arm, shouting down the hall at them.

"We know!" they yelled back. I bet they rolled their eyes at each other. Mary-Kate always panic-cleaned and cooked when someone far out came to visit, and it annoyed the ones living close. They don't understand the excitement of the children you don't see every week coming to visit, because they were all young. Someday, though, I reckon they'll feel guilty for all the moaning about their mother making a fuss when it's their kids coming a long way for a visit.

"We know," Mary-Kate mimicked them, "as if they didn't all get a fruit cake while I was making one for John. Joseph, will you be sure to check there's enough fuel, and get Billy to get some if there isn't. John means well offering to give towards stuff around the house, but I know Dublin is so expensive and I feel so guilty when he spends money on us." I heaved myself up with my two sticks to head out the back, knowing better than to leave Mary-Kate waiting.

"I know."

"Piggy over there wants to take us out for dinner tomorrow night." Billy brought in the two plates of sandwiches for John's kids. Usually, I preferred for food to be eaten at the kitchen table, but Mary-Kate and a team of daughters and daughters-in-law had taken over the kitchen, so I was hiding in front of the television set with the boys.

"Billy, you have children and your own house now, lad, do grow up." In true Billy fashion, John was not getting away with the mild infection that made a good amount of the left side of his face a pale pink. A pale piggy pink, to quote Billy.

"Sounds like a lot of fuss, what does your mother think?"

"She's happy to go."

"Grand so."

"More than fifty years of marriage and she still decides?" He wagged his eyebrows at me. "And I get told to grow up."

"What's a 'prod', Granddad?" John's eldest, Michael, turned to look up at me.

"Excuse me?"

"It's just I got called a 'prod' at school, and when I asked Mam and Dad, they said tell them to grow up, but not what it meant. When you said that to Uncle Billy, it reminded me, can you tell me? Cause they won't." I looked over at Billy confused; he was looking down at Michael quite sad.

"It's short for Protestant, and they say it because Thompson is a Protestant name." Billy looked over at me, a bit guilty. "People wouldn't talk to you back then because of all the anger. But we all got it in school for being Catholics with Protestant names. With everything up the North at the minute and all the trouble up there, the name calling and dirty looks are starting again." The time I spent in the second war hid more from me than my children growing up. Again, the guilt of everything my family went through while I was gone hit. Stay and we had no money, go and I wasn't here to defend them from their heritage. Now that

I thought of it, I didn't know if any more of my children had ended up with lifelong scars like Eliza had. The longer I mulled it over, the more I wondered if I really wanted to ask.

"Why does it matter if I am Catholic, though? I have my Communion next year." Michael had abandoned his sandwiches to give myself and Billy his full attention.

"It shouldn't matter for you, pet. You're a kid. You don't pick sides in all the boring adult politics, do you?" He made a face and shook his head at me. "Well, the short version is, there's lots of fighting going on up the North at the moment, that's nothing to do with you, but you've an English surname, so your classmates and their mammies and daddies make judgements and assume because of your English name you're British, so they're being mean to you."

"But we're Irish."

"I know, but because of all the fighting at the moment."

"But that's nothing to do with me!"

"Michael, you asked, and Grandad is explaining. Don't interrupt." Billy resembled my father a lot when he was being serious.

"Well, there was a lot of fighting and there still is. That's all you need to know right now; you'll learn about it in history class someday. Point is, you're a kid and it shouldn't matter, but people will expect you to be one thing because of your name. Learn some patience, like all your aunties and uncles."

"Okay," he shrugged. The simpler you keep it with kids, the better it is, and there is no need to teach them name-calling and hatred at such a young age. I looked at Billy.

"Even I'm sick of being presumed guilty by people I grew up with." He sat back in the chair.

"It won't go, son, I still get it. Why do you think I stay all the way out here being bossed about by your mother?" Billy laughed.

"Don't act like that's why you follow her around this house, pandering to her every demand and want, Dad. As old as you are, you still look at her like you did when I was a kid. You're, as the Americans would say, whipped, old man." He winked and scooped up our mugs. "Now, keep me in your prayers, I'm gonna brave the Thompson-woman-infested kitchen for the sake of refilling your tea. Come save me if I yell 'biscuit' three times down the hall, boys. Your grandad is too old, they'll suck him in if he comes." He backed out the sitting room, eyes wide, whisper-yelling. He left the room in true Billy Thompson fashion, dramatically and leaving the people behind him in stitches of laughter.

18.

5 April 1975

Her hands were ice-cold in mine. Still as small and delicate as the first time I had ever held them, but ice-cold. No amount of layering her in my gloves, breathing onto them or rubbing them in mine would warm them back up again this time.

"Bye, Nana." Her oldest grandchild kissed her cheek, and then went to join Sandra in the sitting room with all the others who had said goodbye. Kitty was sitting with the parish priest in the kitchen. He had come to give her last rites, and then she asked him to leave. She told him family came before any religion in this house, and while it was a comfort for him to call, she only wanted us with her as she went.

"Goodbye, pet." She leaned back further onto my shoulder. Her lips were slowly getting paler and paler as her heart began to get even slower. Even though our bedroom had felt so big and spacious these last few years, it was crammed now with our twelve children standing around, waiting. Bonnie was in silent hysterics under Billy's arm, Simon stood alone in a corner, dealing by himself. For once, Hazel did not have a cigarette in her hand, instead, she had Thomas' hand in her left and Anthony's in her right. Eliza was trying to be strong and kept together, but was holding John's hand behind her back. Looking around at all of our children, all adults most with their own children, I felt so happy and at peace. In that moment, I thought how my parents must have felt. They did not get the luxury of their children gathering around them for one last goodbye. They only had me... me and my Mary-Kate.

There were no more words said that night. Everything had already been said. She had been in this bed for three days now, slowly fading away from me, and everyone had gotten their moment to talk in private. We didn't need to reassure each other with any last goodbyes, promises or memories. The testament to our love dated fifty years, one war and twelve children. She was dressed in an old dress, older than our marriage, that she had put away out of fond memories, and wrapped in her favourite daisy shawl.

When she let out that final light breath and became still in my arms for good, some had to leave as not to disturb her with their sobbing, and others stood for a few moments with silent tears. I stayed with her as long as I could and felt it rip away— you don't love someone as I did Mary-Kate and not entirely piece your soul together with theirs. That night, in spirit and in mind, I felt I had died with my wife.

I could not speak at her funeral.

I could not be the father who consoled his children.

And when they asked me later, I could not tell my growing grandchildren stories about her.

I felt they saw it in me, though, my family. They left me be and did not disturb me after. When I threw the first hand of clay onto her coffin, a strange feeling of being lost settled over me. Not that I no longer knew where I was, or what I was to do anymore. I could manage to move about my house. But the feeling in my chest of that missing piece, that lost part; my soul that had flown away with hers that night, off to what I hoped was some place of comfort and eternity.

And so, I began my wait, the wait to someday have my mind and memories reunited with her. What was the point in pretending to try and live without her when my whole life had become her? I waited to be brought back to my soul, to my Mary-Kate.

Epilogue.

Joe Thompson did lose multiple brothers in the first world war.

Joe Thompson did in fact fight in both world wars, having to enlist the second time for employment.

He did convert for his wife.

He suffered awfully from frostbite and did end up having amputations.

He was a tailor.